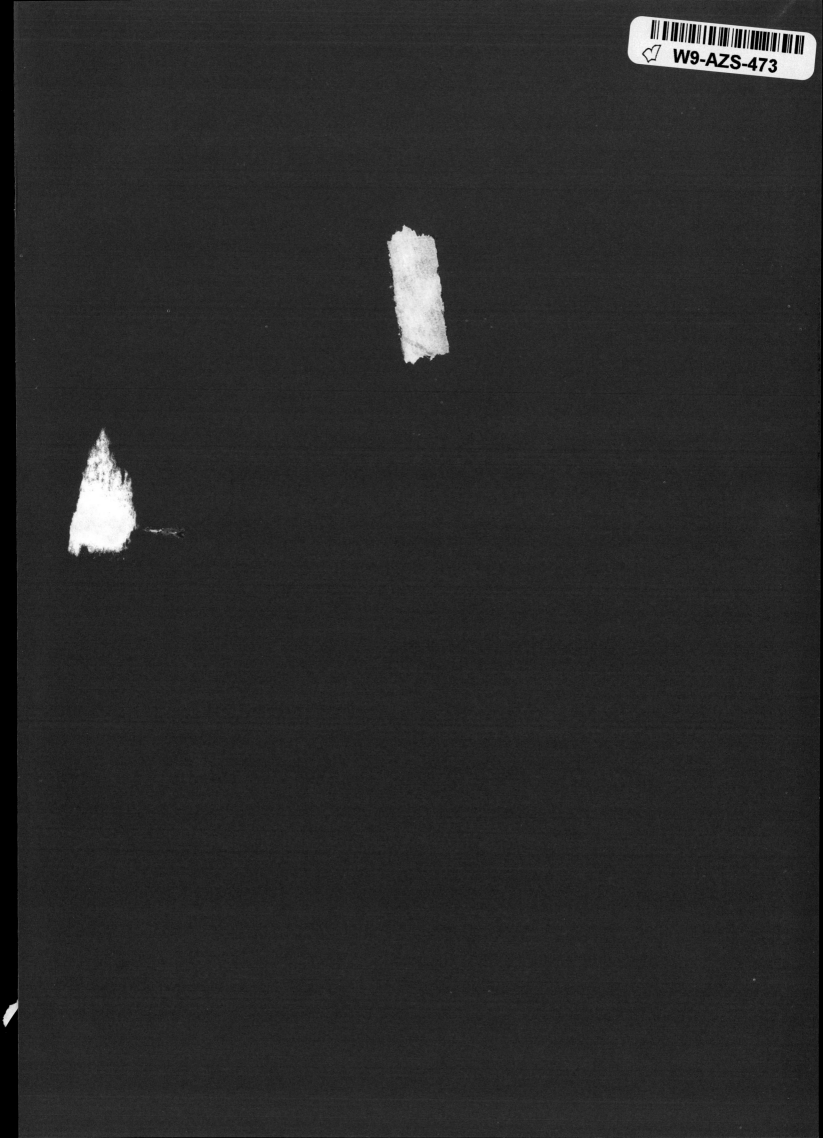

GREAT GENERALS
OF THE
CIVIL WAR
AND THEIR BATTLES

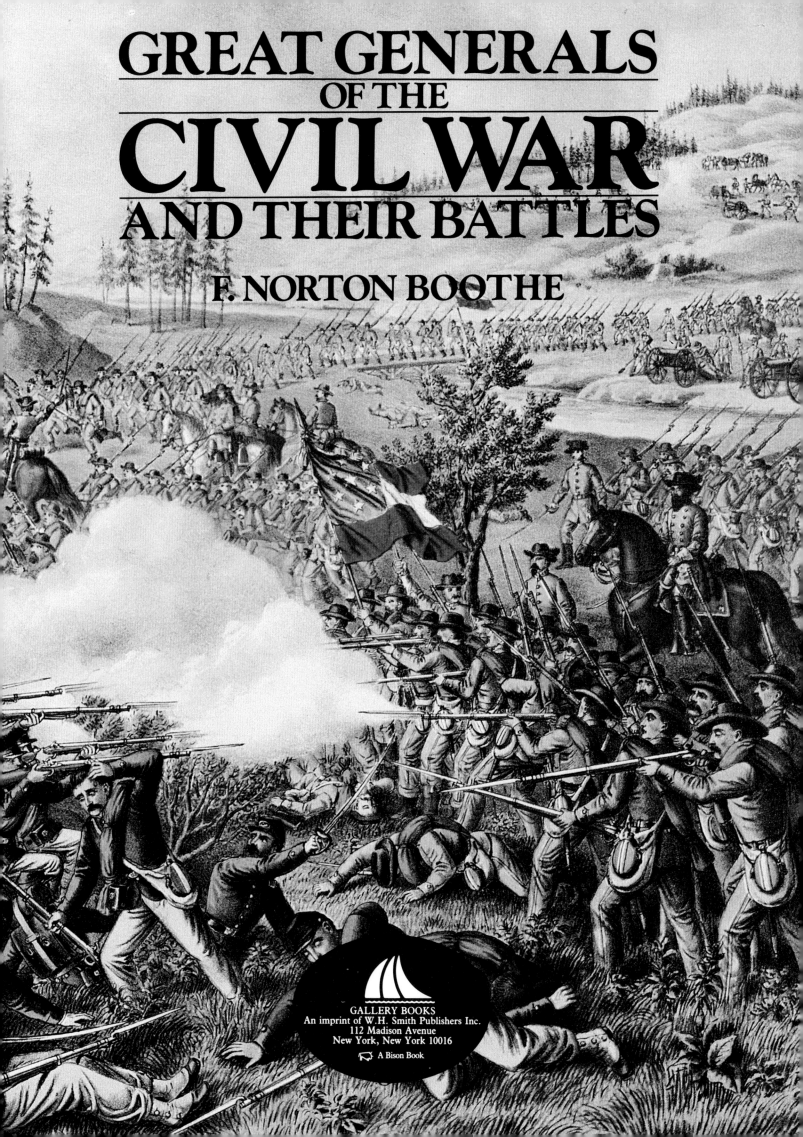

GREAT GENERALS
OF THE
CIVIL WAR
AND THEIR BATTLES

F. NORTON BOOTHE

GALLERY BOOKS
An imprint of W.H. Smith Publishers Inc.
112 Madison Avenue
New York, New York 10016

A Bison Book

Published by Gallery Books
A Division of W H Smith Publishers Inc.
112 Madison Avenue
New York, New York 10016

Produced by
Bison Books Corp.
17 Sherwood Place
Greenwich, CT 06830

ISBN 0-8317-4013-2

Printed in Hong Kong

1 2 3 4 5 6 7 8 9 10

CONTENTS

Previous pages: Union and
Confederate forces engage
in the Battle of
Chickamauga, 1863.

This page: Pickett's Charge
at the Battle of Gettysburg
on 3 July 1863.

THOMAS J JACKSON

First and Second Manassas
Valley Campaign

Fierce combat at Second
Manassas, 30 August 1862.

Above: A sketch of Fort Sumter before it was bombarded by Union land and naval batteries in August 1863, more than two years after its capture by Confederate forces.

Below: The first Union casualty of the war: Elmer Ellsworth died in an attempt to remove a Confederate flag from a hotel roof in Virginia.

H ad either side, the Union or the Confederacy, had its way, there would have been no 'great generals' to emerge from the conflict we know as the Civil War. For both sides wished for one quick and overwhelming victory that would force the opposing government to negotiate a peace. Unfortunately, what came of an initial clash between two opposing views of what constituted states' rights was a war that was fought so long, in so many bloody engagements, and with such intensity that both sides were given the circumstances to produce a number of truly great generals. The first of these to emerge was a man few, if any, of his fellow officers would have predicted possible of greatness – Thomas Jonathan 'Stonewall' Jackson.

He was not the first hero of the war – a role not necessarily the same as that of a great general. For the Confederacy that honor went to General Pierre Gustave Toutant Beauregard, who simply had this mantle fall upon him by virtue of being asked to start firing on Fort Sumter. The North's first hero, meanwhile, was Ephraim Elmer Ellsworth, who on 24 May 1861, after tearing down a Confederate flag flying over a hotel in Alexandria, was shot by the irate proprietor.

In the early weeks of the conflict a number of minor engagements were fought, and each side began to claim its victories and heroes: the North could claim the rout at Philippi on 3 June as the first battle and *their* win, while the South would point to the engagement at Big Bethel on 10 June as the first battle and *their* victory. But the first truly major battle of the war – the one that each side assumed would force the other to sue for peace – was near the railroad junction of Manassas, along the Bull Run Creek, barely a day's march southwest of Washington, DC, and some 85 miles due north of Richmond.

President Jefferson Davis and his top military adviser, General Robert E Lee, had immediately recognized the importance of holding a vital railroad junction such as Manassas and had sent General Beauregard there with a force of some 22,000 men. Another Confederate army of about 12,000 men had been assigned to General Joseph E Johnston to guard against the approach of Union forces from the Shenandoah Valley off to the west. In late June Johnston concentrated his troops at Winchester to be in a better position to support Beauregard while still guarding against the Federal approach. Among Johnston's brigade leaders was a newly appointed brigadier general, Thomas J Jackson. On 16 July, against the better judgment of experienced military men, General Irvin McDowell set out from Washington with a force of about 30,000 men, under orders from President Lincoln to drive Beauregard out of Manassas, and then move on to take Richmond.

Had McDowell struck against Beauregard's force immediately after arriving opposite Manassas Junction, he might well have routed the Confederates. But as was to happen throughout this war, a commander delayed. This allowed Johnston the time he needed to move his forces from Winchester – most of them coming by railroad in the first such use of this relatively new technology – so that by the morning of 21 July Johnston's force was there to support Beauregard. It was significant that the first of Johnston's brigades to arrive at Manassas Junction was that led by General Jackson. The battle that occurred that day was also a harbinger of many of the battles to come in that it was a compound of bravery and errors, of opportunities missed and accidents exploited, of sound generalship and sheer guts. But one thing was sure during this First Battle at Manassas: Jackson's brigade played a crucial role.

Left: A trainload of Confederate troops on the way to Manassas. Families and wives bid them farewell.

Below: General Thomas J Jackson and the Stonewall Brigade at the First Battle of Bull Run, 21 July 1861.

Jackson himself had selected the position to rally the Confederate troops who were being driven back by the Federal enveloping movement on their left flank. It was a prominence known as Henry House Hill, and here Jackson aligned his brigade and set up the guns. Whenever the Confederates moved out against the Federals, the latter proved too strong and drove them back to Henry House Hill. For a while it appeared that the Federals were going to push the Rebels right off that hill, but Jackson's brigade absorbed the charge – and the casualties – and inspired the other Confederate troops in the area to stop the advancing Federals. It was at this point in the battle that he acquired the nickname that would characterize him to the world ever after.

General Barnard E Bee, another of the Confederate brigade commanders, had been running up and down the lines, trying to encourage his men to repel the enemy, but with no success – his brigade was reduced to a mere handful. Riding up to Jackson, he said, 'General, they are beating us back.' Jackson replied, 'Sir, we'll give them the bayonet.' Bee managed then to rally what was left of his troops and cry out to them, 'There is Jackson standing like a stone wall. Let us determine to die here, and we will conquer.' His men did rally behind him; Bee was mortally wounded a few minutes after. The incident was reported graphically in the press, and the name caught the public imagination. From then on Jackson was 'Stonewall,' and the brigade he commanded proudly became known as the Stonewall Brigade. It was at First Manassas also that Jackson gave rise to another legend that was to bedevil the Union

soldiers right down to the end of the war. In the midst of the fiercest fighting Jackson ordered his men: 'Reserve your fire till they come within fifty yards, then fire and give them the bayonet; and when you charge, yell like furies!' The habit spread through the Southern army, and from that day on the 'Rebel yell' became a familiar sound on the battlefield.

With the arrival of fresh Confederate troops and the shift of units on the spot, the Confederates, with General Jackson now taking the lead on the offensive, soon forced the Federals to retreat. Only their own exhaustion, disorder and inexperience kept the Confederates from pursuing the Union army all the way back to Wash-

Top: Robert E Lee (white hair) and his generals. Stonewall Jackson is farthest to the right.

Above: Portraits of Jefferson Davis (left), Confederate President, and Abraham Lincoln, United States President.

ington. But as both sides retired to regroup their forces, one thing was clear: the heroes of Manassas were Jackson's brigade – and, above all, Stonewall Jackson, its intrepid commander. What few people knew at the time was just how unusual, even eccentric, a man this was. For although Jackson was a native of Virginia and a graduate of West Point, he had little else in common with many of the other Confederate commanders who would achieve greatness – such men as Lee, Johnston, or Stuart.

Thomas Jonathan Jackson was born on 21 January 1824 in Clarksburg, a frontier settlement in the mountains of western Virginia, a region where blunt honesty and self-reliance were inbred qualities. Orphaned by the age of six – his father died when he was two, his mother four years later – Thomas Jackson, with his beloved younger sister Laura, grew up in the home of their kindly and indulgent bachelor uncle, Cummins Jackson. Though rather a slow learner in school, Thomas was untiring and persistent in applying himself to his studies, and never forgot what he learned. In 1842, at the age of 22, he was granted an appointment to the US Military Academy at West Point, where he arrived in homespun clothes, with a pair of weatherbeaten saddlebags over his shoulder and a coarse felt hat pulled rather ludicrously over his head. Even then he was unconcerned about his appearance or what others might think of it. He was what he was, and, as he once long after explained to a friend, 'I have no gift for *seeming*. His gift, it appears, was for *being*, and at an early age he showed an integrity unusual for his years.

Top: Soldier-artist Samuel J Reader's rendering of *Rebels Riding into the Line of Battle*.

Above: Confederate flags, top to bottom – the National flag; the Stars and Bars; the Battle flag.

Left: Reader's depiction titled, *Kill the Yanks – Shoot Them*.

Though lacking the advantages of a good early education and the propensity to excel as a student, Jackson succeeded, with relentless effort and self-discipline astounding to his fellow cadets, in graduating with a standing of 17th in his class of 59. (His classmates paid him a tribute of sorts in claiming he would have stood first in his class had they stayed a fifth year.) His high standing earned him his choice of services, and as Brevet 2nd Lieutenant he embarked upon his requested assignment in the artillery. Before long he was on his way to join in the campaign General Winfield Scott was waging in Mexico. With the cool confidence that was to mark his later engagements in battle, Jackson planned and executed a brilliant feat with artillery in the storming of Chapultepec, and, just 15 months after his graduation from West Point, he received glowing praise for gallantry from Scott and the rank of Brevet Major. In Mexico he learned what the books he had pored over at the Military Academy had neglected – the value of strategy and tactics and careful logistic planning. And Thomas Jackson never forgot what he learned!

When the war ended Jackson stayed on in Mexico City, as did many other US Army officers, undertook the study of Spanish, and was awakened by the omnipresence of churches and clergy around him to an innate interest in religion

that was to grow into one of the two main dedications in his life – the other being a total commitment to duty, especially duty to his country. He seems to have considered no career except the army, and subsequently was posted to Fort Meade in Florida, presumably to keep down the depredations of Seminole Indians. Actually, Jackson found he was spending his time at a desk with no more hostility in the area than that of interoffice feuding. In the midst of this situation he received an invitation from the Virginia Military Institute in Lexington, Virginia, asking if he would be interested in the position of professor of natural and experimental philosophy and artillery tactics. The position offered considerable prestige and a fair salary for a junior officer in the army in peacetime. Being personally involved in the regimen of an institution run along the same lines as the US Military Academy appealed to Jackson. He would continue to live the life of an officer, with its discipline and duty, and have a part in actively training boys who would one day perhaps be officers. It also meant returning to his native Virginia, indeed, to that region of it so familiar to him from his early years. It was an offer he could not refuse.

Though he was only 27 years old when he went to VMI, Jackson soon became known among the boys as 'Old Jack' because of his austere manner

A formal portrait of Thomas Jonathan Jackson with his family. This mezzotint was engraved by William Sartain and published in 1866. Pictured here are Jackson's second wife, Mary Anna Morrison, who he married in 1857, and the daughter she bore in 1861, Julia Laura.

and eccentric ways. He adhered to a rigid diet of plain food from which he never, even on celebrative occasions, departed. (Actually, Jackson had long suffered from a chronic digestive ailment, which he sensibly controlled by prudence in what he ate.) In the classroom he was intolerant of any breach of discipline, and he displayed what must have seemed to the boys as a spinsterish love of order and method. He had a habit of sitting ramrod straight in a chair – one he had formed at West Point, incidentally, believing it placed less strain on the alimentary system. His appearance was at best unprepossessing; he was attired always in the same prescribed uniform with his cap pulled down over his eyes. (It so happened that he had eye troubles that made him especially sensitive to light.) There was one cadet, at least, Leigh Wilber Reid, who recognized in the reserved and awkward teacher, in his very mode of life, something transcending the walls of VMI and the polite society of Lexington. He expressed it in a poem he addressed to 'Alias Hickory, Alias Old Jack.' Its first four lines seem almost precognitive:

Like some rough brute, that ranged the forest wild
So rude, uncouth, so purely Nature's child
Is Hickory, and yet methinks I see
The stamp of genius on his brow.

As curious as Jackson may have appeared to the ever-critical young and the more social circles of Lexington, there was one place in town where he was totally in his rightful element. It was the Presbyterian church. The interest in religion that

had first stirred in him during his months in Mexico City had over the years deepened to a sustaining belief and faith that pervaded every aspect of his life. Not that he paraded his religiosity, or could be called in any sense a fanatic, simply that it was essential to his existence. He developed the habit of accompanying every act, however trivial or customary, with a silent prayer. As a deacon in the church, he organized a Sunday School for black children, concerned lest they be left out of Christian instruction, and both financed and led it himself. (He himself owned no slaves, nor did he ascribe to the institution of slavery.) The first thing he did the very day after the victory at First Manassas was to send a note to the Reverend William S White, pastor of his church in Lexington, not about the outcome of the battle, but enclosing his check for 'our colored Sunday-school.'

As the war between the South and North seemed ever more imminent, he felt that the crisis might be avoided if all united in prayer. About war he had once said: 'I have seen enough of it to make me look upon it as the sum of all evils.' He had also said: 'If I know myself, all I am and all I have are at the service of my country.' When war between the states was finally declared he felt, according to the creed in which he had been reared, that his country was, first, his native state. Like Robert E Lee, he felt he had no choice. On the eve of the outbreak of hostilities, the superintendent of VMI called the cadets together and talked to them about law and order in the hope of checking any impetuous action on

Prayer in Stonewall Jackson's camp. Jackson stands in the rear left with an orderly and a servant to his right. Sitting in the foreground is Lieutenant General A P Hill; standing and facing Jackson is Lieutenant General R S Ewell; and kneeling is Lieutenant Colonel A J Pendleton.

Pages 14-15: Confederate troops salute Stonewall Jackson, mounted on a black horse, at Chancellorsville.

Uniforms of the Confederate Army. Left to right: infantry; regular Confederate troops; cavalry; artillery; Louisiana Zouaves; Washington artillery of New Orleans; Mississippi Rifles; heavy infantry of Georgia; Alabama light infantry; and Marine battery, Manassas Junction.

their part. As Jackson entered the assembly hall the cadets, rather jokingly, called for 'Jackson, Jackson, Old Jack.' At first he declined to address them. Urged by the superintendent, Colonel Francis H Smith, to do so, Jackson rose and took the rostrum, looking taller than his 5 feet, 10 inches. With his usually absent-minded eyes flashing a fiery light, he said: 'The time for war has not yet come, but it will come, and that soon; and when it does come, my advice is to draw the sword and throw away the scabbard.' The Presbyterian deacon had become Joshua storming the walls of Jericho.

Four days after that assembly and Jackson's brief speech, Virginia seceded from the Union. The Institute went on a war footing. The cadets were ordered to move to Richmond. Jackson, the senior officer present for duty, was put in charge of the marching column. It was his first command in the war that would make him a hero and a legend.

On 1 May Jackson was sent to head up the Virginian force that had seized Harper's Ferry, considered of strategic importance because of its location on the edge of the Shenandoah Valley as well as for its arsenal. General Joseph E Johnston arrived there on 23 May to assume command of the newly formed Confederate Army. Johnston soon organized the troops in the Army of the Shenandoah under four brigades, one commanded by Jackson. It was this unit, imbued with the discipline he soon instilled in them and their dedication to him and readiness to obey his every order, that became the Stonewall Brigade at First Manassas.

After the jubilation that swept the Confederacy in the wake of the victory at First Manassas, Jackson retired from the public stage; indeed, General Beauregard was widely regarded as the hero of Manassas. Jackson was relieved to be out of the limelight. He had a formidable task ahead – strengthening his troops, many of them little more than boys straight off the farm, and conditioning them by rigorous training to be ready for whatever lay ahead. He was a strict disciplinarian, and allowed himself no special privileges he refused his men. And with his aloof, taciturn manner, absence of humor, and peculiar habit of continually sucking a lemon, he some-

times impressed those around him as odd to the point of being perhaps plain crazy. Yet his men came to love him, to be willing to follow him to the death, with that devotion few commanders have ever been given. He was for real, and they knew it.

In October 1861 Jackson was promoted to the rank of major general and assigned to command one of the newly formed districts under the Department of Northern Virginia – the Shenandoah Valley District. The Shenandoah Valley extends on a northeast-southwest axis for some 100 miles between the Blue Ridge and Allegheny Mountains in northwest Virginia. Aside from being regarded as a potential invasion route between the North and the South, it was extremely fertile and productive and would be valued by Virginians throughout the Civil War as their major source of food. When Jackson arrived there, he immediately set about trying to organize the mostly militia units, but by November he was assigned what he insisted he needed, his old Stonewall Brigade. Through his usual attention to detail, Jackson turned his mixed forces into a respectable army of 10,000 men, though unable to do much during the winter of 1861-62 against the superior Federal forces, led by General Nathaniel Banks along the Potomac and General William Rosecrans in western Virginia. It was during this period, in January 1862, that Jackson became so frustrated by the interference of the Confederate Secretary of War in one of his command assignments that he threatened to resign from the army; Richmond backed away, and Jackson continued in command.

By early March Banks had crossed the Potomac into the Shenandoah Valley to force Jackson to evacuate the town of Winchester. As the much larger Federal forces began to take over the northern end of the Valley, still other Federal forces to the east were threatening a campaign in the Virginia Peninsula. Jackson knew his immediate mission was to hold as many Federal troops in the Valley as possible, and when it was reported on the 21st that large numbers were on the move eastward, Jackson made a forced march. Jackson's cavalry commander was the dashing Colonel Turner Ashby, and after he made his first attack on the Federal forces on

Saturday, the 22nd, he informed Jackson that there was only a small rear guard of Federals in the area around Kernstown. Jackson's religious scruples usually forbade him to fight on Sunday, but the urgency of the situation persuaded him to launch an attack on the 23rd against what turned out to be a Federal force of 9000 men. Jackson's 4200 men were so totally outnumbered that they were soon close to being wiped out; Jackson got away with his wounded and supplies, and only Ashby's cavalry prevented the pursuing Federals from turning Kernstown into an even greater disaster. Ironically, though, such was Jackson's reputation as an astute commander that the Federals assumed he would never have chosen to attack unless he had a much larger force somewhere on call, so the Union army not only kept Banks's troops in the Valley, but the Federals sent reinforcements and generally revised their strategy.

During April Jackson had to retreat down the Valley in the face of the overwhelmingly larger Federal forces led by General Banks. By 26 April the Federals' main force was at New Market, with an outpost still farther south at Harrisonburg. Jackson had taken a stand at Swift Run Gap, east and south of there, and with reinforcements from General Richard S Ewell he had now had some 17,000 men at his command. Meanwhile, Federal General John Frémont was now threatening to move in from the Allegheny Mountains to the west and join up with Banks's force. Jackson knew this would prove fatal, so with Lee's authorization to proceed as he saw fit, he left Richard

A photographic portrait of General Richard S Ewell, whose troops reinforced Jackson at Swift Run Gap in the Shenandoah Valley Campaign.

Ewell's division of some 8000 at Swift Run Gap and led his own division and Ashby's cavalry farther south into the Valley, then crossed the mountains to the west, and confronted the totally confused Federal forces at McDowell on the edge of the Allegheny Mountains. Jackson's troops had now marched 92 miles in four days, one of several such forced marches under Jackson that earned his troops the dubious honour of being called 'foot cavalry.' On 8 May they repulsed the main attack of Federal forces (although the Confederates suffered 498 casualties, almost twice as many as the Union's). Jackson even pursued the retreating Federals westward to Franklin, in what was soon to be West Virginia, but on 13 May he returned to McDowell.

Left: An engraving of General Thomas J Jackson in a pensive pose. A deeply religious man, Jackson reconciled his convictions with his duty.

Right: Union General N B Banks, who was driven out of the Shenandoah Valley by Jackson.

By this time Jackson was well aware that his main strength lay in his mobility. After all, the Federals had three large armies that singly or together might have overwhelmed his force in any conventional battle. Frémont's army still threatened from the western edge of the Allegheny Mountains; Banks's army still dominated the northern half of the Shenandoah Valley; and off to the east sat the forces of Union General Irvin McDowell at Fredericksburg. So Jackson wasted no time and on 14 May set off again, this time heading north back up the Valley. When he got to a small mountain range, the Massanuttens, lying between the Blue Ridge and the Alleghenies, he cut across it to the east, joined up with General Ewell's force at Luray, and then proceeded straight toward the Federals at Front Royal. General Banks had not expected this shift and had assigned only 1000 Federals to Front Royal; Jackson now was leading a force of 16,000. Assisting matters further, the charming, 17-year-old Belle Boyd, who lived in the region and liked nothing more than spying, informed Jackson's advance unit of the Union troop movements, enabling it to attack even before Jackson arrived on the scene.

In the action on that 23 May, the Federals had 904 of their 1063 men killed, wounded, or captured, while Jackson's men took only some 50 casualties. When Banks heard of this disaster, he withdrew his main force north up the Valley to Winchester, which Jackson had abandoned in March. Jackson pushed his by now exhausted troops north in pursuit of Banks's force. He himself seemed capable of almost superhuman exertions, but many of his men found the march through the night of 24-25 May almost the breaking point. As one of Jackson's subordinates later wrote: 'he forgot that others were differently constituted, and paid little heed to commissariat [i.e. food]; but woe to the man who failed to bring up the ammunition!' Jackson had good reason to push his troops; he knew that if Banks had time to dig in on the high ground at Winchester, it would be very hard to force the Federals out.

Union General John Charles Fremont was defeated by Stonewall Jackson in the Shenandoah Valley campaign in western Virginia. Fremont, a flashy figure who took a radical antislavery stance, was later placed under General Pope but refused to serve and was relieved in June 1862.

Opposite: Seventeen-year-old Belle Boyd aided Stonewall Jackson's Valley Campaign by spying for the Confederates and reporting Union intentions.

Once again Jackson had to mount an attack on Sunday, and at dawn on the 25th he moved out against the Federals. At first the Union artillery and cavalry were able to hold off the Confederates, but Jackson sent units to both the right and left flanks and then, about seven in the morning, all the Confederate elements began to advance. The Federals were able to resist at first, but soon were routed. On the 26th Banks took his defeated army back across the Potomac: in the last three days he had lost about 3000 men out of the 8500 under his command, while Jackson's losses had been only some 400. Far more crucial, though, was the fact that Jackson's string of victories forced the Union to revise its strategy, which had, of course, been the purpose of the whole Valley Campaign. In the east General George McClellan had launched a full-blown Federal attack on the Peninsula, with the intention of reaching Richmond and forcing its surrender. Lee and Jackson were in constant, and carefully guarded, communication about this operation, and agreed that Jackson must keep the Union forces busy in the Valley to siphon off troops that could perhaps help McClellan achieve his goal. Their diversionary tactic did just what it was supposed to do. Instead of pressing the attack on Richmond, Lincoln and his advisers decided they must concentrate their main efforts on subduing Jackson, whom they now perceived as in a position to threaten Washington itself. General John

Frémont was ordered to bring his force into the Valley and McDowell to bring his corps over from Fredericksburg. They were to converge on Strasburg, south of Winchester, so that when Banks moved back down from the north again, Jackson's force would be trapped from the rear.

Jackson soon learned of the movements of the Federals and on 30 May began to withdraw his main force southward, leaving his famed Stonewall Brigade to hold off Banks to the north. As Jackson was riding on a train ahead of his troops, a courier stopped it and informed him that McDowell's advance unit had already recaptured Front Royal. With his force of 16,000 men stretched thin along the Valley and some 50,000 Federals converging on his escape route, Jackson might well have panicked. Instead, he coolly ordered his cavalry under Turner Ashby to check Frémont's advance from the west and sent one brigade of infantry to hold off the advance force of McDowell's army from the east. On 1 June Jackson was able to get his now intact force, plus 2000 prisoners and a double wagontrain that stretched some seven miles, out of Strasburg and thus elude the trap. Jackson moved south into the Valley, with Ashby protecting his rear against Federal attacks, and had his men destroy as many bridges as possible so that the pursuing Federals would be delayed. On 6 June Jackson's force suffered a major loss when General Turner Ashby was killed in an engagement near Harrisonburg.

A night scene at the rendezvous of Colonel Mosby and his men in the pass of the Blue Ridge Mountains, Shenandoah Valley, Virginia.

Jackson was devastated when he received the news. He locked himself alone in his room and was heard pacing the floor for hours. Ashby, like 'Jeb' Stuart, for whom Jackson also had an especially warm feeling, was one of those young Southern gentlemen of leisure who, at the war's outbreak, joined the cavalry and made a name for themselves in history and the hearts of friend and foe alike by their deeds of rash bravery of the kind rarely encountered outside the pages of a romantic novel. Though so completely the contrary of his commanding officer – unruly, incapable of discipline with his men, often rash in judgment and in action – he won Jackson's indulgence of his ways and profound respect. Jackson would explain why in an account he wrote after Ashby's death: 'His daring was proverbial; his powers of endurance almost incredible; his tone of character heroic, and his sagacity almost intuitive in divining the purposes and movements of the enemy.' The entire Confederacy mourned the loss of this gallant cavalier. His troopers cried openly at his funeral.

Jackson had made plans to take a stand at Port Republic. He had his faithful map-maker, Jebediah 'Jed' Hotchkiss, prepare a detailed map of the surrounding country. (Jackson was among the first to realize the importance to a general of expertly drawn maps, and he had sought the services of Hotchkiss early on in the Valley Campaign. At that time the entire region was virtually uncharted territory, with little more than local inhabitants to direct anyone from one spot to another.) An advance brigade from McDowell's army got into Port Republic, and Jackson was almost captured in a skirmish on 8 June. Realizing that the two Federal forces were now close to converging, Jackson chose not to retreat. Instead, he assigned Ewell to take on Frémont's force of about 12,000 at Cross Keys, or Union Church, west of Port Republic; Ewell's men held back the superior numbers all day on the 8th. Then, on the next day, Ewell left a small force to face Frémont's men and took the bulk of his men over to the east side of Port Republic to confront the advance elements of McDowell's army. The Stonewall Brigade launched the attack on the morning of the 9th, and because Ewell's forces were delayed in arriving, for awhile the Confederates were seriously threatened with almost total destruction. But Ewell's men finally arrived, and by 11:00 that morning the Federals began to pull back. Frémont, meanwhile, had pushed the small force of Confederates back, but because they had burned the bridge behind them, Frémont could not get across in time to help McDowell's men.

In these two days of fighting at Cross Keys and Port Republic Jackson's total force of some 16,000 men had suffered about 1100 casualties while the Federals had taken about 1700 casualties out of their 17,000 men engaged. Although the Federal forces ringing the Shenandoah Valley

An etching from *Frank Leslie's Illustrated Newspaper* (28 June 1862) captioned, 'The gallant attack by 150 of the Pennsylvania Bucktails, led by Colonel Kane, upon a portion of General Stonewall Jackson's rebel army, consisting of cavalry, infantry and artillery, strongly posted in the woods near Harrisonburg, Friday, June 7.'

Right: A picket on the Chickahominy, with relief approaching.

Below: A Remington Zouave percussion lock rifle musket. The percussion lock, first used in the Mexican War, became common in the Civil War.

Bottom: A Confederate powder flask.

were still vastly superior to Jackson's, such was his reputation now in Washington as well as in the field that the Union decided to leave him alone, at least for awhile. In so doing, the Federals recognized the effectiveness of Jackson's own principles of warfare: 'Always mystify, mislead, and surprise the enemy, if possible; and when you strike and overcome him, never let up in the pursuit so long as your men have strength to follow; for an army routed, if hotly pursued, becomes panick-stricken, and can then be destroyed by half their number. The other rule is, never fight against heavy odds, if by any possible maneuvering you can hurl your own force on only a part, and that the weakest part, of your enemy and crush it. Such tactics will win every time, and a small army may thus destroy a large one in detail, and repeated victory will make it invincible.'

Jackson proposed to Lee that he be allowed to pursue Banks's force all the way up the Valley and possibly into Maryland and Pennsylvania. Lee had more pressing need of him elsewhere, however. He ordered him to bring his men to help in disposing of the Federal army under McClellan that was threatening Richmond along the Chickahominy River. Maintaining the strictest secrecy about his direction and purpose, Jackson moved his troops out of the Valley toward their rendezvous with the Army of Northern Virginia, a long and arduous journey for men who had been tramping up and down the Valley for weeks, covering hundreds of miles, with little sleep, minimum rations, and rugged terrain. This final, unforeseen trek, often beginning at 2:30 AM, came close to breaking their endurance. Jackson himself went four days with only ten hours' sleep, and arrived at his destination in a wet, mud-caked uniform, benumbed by over a hundred

miles in the saddle, gaunt from lack of food. That the performance of him and his men in the Seven Days' Battles was not up to what was expected of them is hardly to be wondered at. It was disappointing, of course, to Lee and his officers, though Lee never joined in the criticism expressed by others. The simple fact was, quite obviously, that Jackson was physically exhausted from the Valley Campaign and the subsequent arduous march, and for the only time in his career became overcautious and even at times indecisive.

In any case, Lee succeeded in pushing McClellan out of the Peninsula, and the Union was forced to come up with a new plan for taking Richmond. Lincoln selected General John Pope to lead an army of 50,000 men south from Washington to seize the railroad junction of Gordonsville, some 50 miles northwest of Richmond. Lee then sent Jackson with a force of about 12,000 men to challenge Pope; at Jackson's request, another 12,000 men under General A P Hill were also assigned to him. On 9 August Jackson confronted a Union force under General Nathaniel Banks at Cedar Mountain, and again Jackson's uncustomary slowness almost cost the Confederates the day, but A P Hill mounted a counterattack and stopped the Federals. During the next two weeks both armies feinted and jabbed at one another from their positions on either side of the Rappahannock River. Meanwhile Lee realized that he had to take some action before Pope was joined by the full force of McClellan's army, now being brought up and around. Lee took a decision that was a page right out of Jackson's own book of warfare: against a force of some 75,000 versus his own 55,000, he decided to send about half of his men in a wide strategic envelopment that would come down onto the Federal line between Pope and Washington. When Pope reacted to that, Lee intended

Below: Union General John Pope (1822-1892).

Below left: A Table of fire for a light 12-pounder gun.

TABLE OF FIRE. LIGHT 12-POUNDER GUN. MODEL 1857.

SHOT. Charge 2¼ Pounds.		SPHERICAL CASE SHOT. Charge 2½ Pounds.			SHELL. Charge 2 Pounds.		
ELEVATION In Degrees.	RANGE In Yards.	ELEVATION In Degrees.	TIME OF FLIGHT. Seconds.	RANGE In Yards.	ELEVATION In Degrees.	TIME OF FLIGHT In Seconds.	RANGE In Yards.
0°	323	0°50'	1"	300	0°	0"'75	300
1°	620	1°	1"75	575	0°30	1"25	425
2°	875	1°30'	2"5	635	1°	1"75	615
3°	1200	2°	3"	730	1°30'	2"25	700
4°	1325	3°	4"	960	2°	2"75	785
5°	1680	3°30'	4"75	1080	2°30'	3"5	925
		3°40'	5"	1135	3°	4"	1080
					3°45'	5"	1300

Use SHOT at masses of troops, and to batter, from 600 up to 2,000 yards.   Use SHELL for firing buildings, at troops posted in woods, in pursuit, and to produce a moral rather than a physical effect; greatest effective range 1,500 yards.   Use SPHERICAL CASE SHOT at masses of troops, at not less than 500 yards; generally up to 1,500 yards.   CANISTER is not effective at 600 yards; it should not be used beyond 500 yards, and but very seldom and over the most favorable ground at that distance; at short ranges, (less than 200 yards,) in emergency, use double canister, with single charge.   Do not employ RICOCHET at less distance than 1,000 to 1,100 yards.

CARE OF AMMUNITION CHEST.

1st. Keep everything out that does not belong in them, except a bunch of cord or wire for breakage; beware of loose tacks, nails, bolts, or scraps.
2d. Keep friction primers in their papers, tied up.   The pouch containing those for instant service must be closed, and so placed as to be secure. Take every precaution that primers do not get loose; a single one may cause an explosion.   Use plenty of tow in packing.

(This sheet is to be glued on to the inside of Limber Chest Cover.)

to commit the other half of his forces. Everything depended on speed and secrecy – and here is where Jackson once again came through.

Jackson set off on 25 August with some 24,000 men and marched them 26 miles; the next day, he pushed them 36 miles; by the evening of the 27th his men had swooped down on the Federal supply depot at Manassas Junction. Pope had at first believed that Jackson was cutting off to the Shenandoah Valley again, but when he heard of the attack at Manassas, he called in all his supporting forces until he had 75,000 men positioned between Lee's divided army. Another more daring general might have struck to wipe out both of these smaller forces, but Pope somehow could not find Jackson's army and seemed to ignore the existence of Lee's other force, led by General James Longstreet. On the night of 27-28 August Lee moved his force into the woods near Groveton, along the road to Centreville. Pope, after receiving a report that Confederates were attacking Centreville, moved up the Warrenton Pike late that afternoon. As the lead division came up, Jackson took yet another daring and unconventional decision: he attacked it with only about a third of his total force at hand. This battle of Groveton, small as it was, took high casualties on both sides, but Jackson was vindicated: the Federals withdrew, and this gave Lee time to get Longstreet closer to Jackson's force.

On the 29th Pope still had the advantage – 62,000 men against Jackson's 20,000 – but Jackson's men were entrenched behind a railroad cut, and Pope's frontal attacks failed to dislodge them. Jackson himself rode up and down his lines, exhorting them to hold on until Longstreet could arrive: 'Half an hour, men, only half an hour; can you stand it half an hour?' When ammunition gave out, the Confederates actually began to hurl rocks at the attacking Federals. About 11 o'clock in the morning Longstreet's force of some 30,000 men finally arrived, but instead of driving straight at the Federal flank, Longstreet simply distracted the Federals attacking Jackson so that the day ended with Jackson's men withdrawing from some of their advance positions.

Pope believed that the Confederates were going to retreat and ordered a full-scale pursuit for the next day. Instead, the Federals came up against a now greatly reinforced Confederate force. Soon Pope's army was almost caught between Jackson's and Longstreet's flanking moves; the Federals got away only because some of their men held the commanding position on Henry House Hill – the very position where Jackson and his brigade had earned their sobriquet 'Stonewall' in the First Battle of Manassas. After a day's rest Lee tried to keep up the offensive and sent Jackson against the west flank of the Federals at Chantilly, near Centreville. The Federals were able to resist fiercely, but two of their generals – Isaac Stevens and Philip Kearney – were killed. Although Pope still greatly outnumbered Lee's army, after this engagement he withdrew his army back to Washington. During this whole Second Manassas Campaign the Union had engaged some 76,000 men, and taken about 16,000 casualties; the Confederates had engaged about 49,000 men, and taken 9200 casualties. Neither side had been free of tactical errors, both had

Artist A R Waud's etching of a scene from the Battle of Cedar Mountain, fought 9 August 1862.

failed to press for the kill. Nevertheless, the Confederates had achieved their immediate goal: they had driven the Union Army out of northern Virginia.

In the months that followed the partnership of Lee and Jackson came to capture the hearts and aspirations of the Confederacy. They complemented one another as though cast in the same mould. Jackson once said, 'Lee is the only man I know whom I would follow blindfold.' And Lee was to say after Jackson's death that 'the sun never shone' on such a commanding officer. Yet

they were never in their relationship as superior and subordinate, rather as equals with a single purpose, each bringing forth the best in the other. Even though they failed in their major objective when they invaded Maryland and fought at Antietam, they gave the South some sense of satisfaction by taking the war that far north, and Jackson himself performed superbly. Promoted to lieutenant general in October 1862, Jackson was now the recipient of gifts from grateful Southerners and praise from newspaper editorials even in foreign lands. When Colonel Garnet Wolseley, later to become commander in chief of the British Army, visited Jackson, he wrote: 'I felt that I had at last solved the mystery of the Stonewall Brigade, and discovered why it was that it had accomplished such almost miraculous feats. With such a leader, men would go anywhere and face any amount of difficulties.'

After participating in the great victory at Fredericksburg on 13 December 1862, Jackson went into winter quarters. He was in fine form for the campaign in April that climaxed at the Battle of Chancellorsville – to become famous as 'a

classic feat in modern warfare,' as the historian Allan Nevins has termed what he considered Lee's most magnificent military victory. In planning, strategy and impetus, Chancellorsville was the product of that model relationship between Lee and Jackson. Together they plotted their movements every step of the way as the battle approached and at last was under way. On the evening of the first day of battle, 1 May 1863, they sat side by side on a fallen log among the pines of a woodland and discussed a maneuver for the next day that would take the Federal general, Joseph Hooker, totally unaware. Jackson was to lead a particularly devious flank march. After they parted, Jackson spread his saddle blanket in a little clearing in the woods. One of his staff officers, Alexander 'Sandie' Pendleton, insisted on giving him his overcoat as a cover. Reluctantly, Jackson consented, on condition that they share it, but long before morning he got up from the cold and clammy ground, spread the coat over Sandie, and joined a group sitting around a courier's fire, hoping to ward off the evident beginnings of a cold.

The fighting went as planned that day, but that evening of 2 May Jackson was not content to leave things be until the morning. He went off on his horse, Little Sorrel, to reconnoiter. In the darkness and confusion because of a few shots believed to come from a possible Federal attack, he was struck from his horse by shots from Confederate soldiers. His left arm was shattered, and he had to be taken from the field to what served as a hospital for amputation, the only means available in that era for dealing with such an injury. The operation was a success; it seemed certain he would recover.

When questioned once by a staff officer during the Valley Campaign about his extraordinary composure in battle, Jackson had responded confidently, 'God has fixed the time for my death.' That time had now come. The cold he had contracted that night on the clammy ground in the woods developed into pneumonia. He died on 10 May — a Sunday. Early that morning he had murmured, 'I have always desired to die on a Sunday.'

Throughout the Confederacy he was mourned as no one had ever been, as few have ever been since. A corps of VMI cadets accompanied his coffin to Lexington, where he was buried as he had wished to be. For Lee, Jackson's death meant more than the loss of a cherished friend and associate. 'I know not how to replace him,' he said, and he was thinking of the fate of the South in its struggle. Posterity would confirm Jackson's reputation as one of the great generals of the Civil War, indeed of all history. His Shenandoah Valley Campaign, in particular, would be constantly analyzed by students of military history in this country and abroad. But in his last words perhaps lay the true Jackson, the restless warrior and the devout Christian: 'Let us cross over the river and rest under the shade of the trees.'

James E B Stuart

Peninsular Campaign
Antietam
Brandy Station

The Battle of Antietam, 17 September 1862.

It was a British cavalry officer of the Napoleonic era who observed, perhaps with some irony, that the purpose of cavalry in warfare was to lend tone to an affair that would otherwise be merely a vulgar brawl. Southern cavalry genius James Ewell Brown 'Jeb' Stuart would certainly have agreed with this observation, though probably without irony. More cynically, Mark Twain once said that the antebellum South lived in a dream world based on the knight-errant novels of Sir Walter Scott. This too seems to catch Jeb Stuart: known to many as The Cavalier, calling himself The Knight of the Golden Spurs, Stuart followed his trade of pursuing enemies as a grand and romantic game out of the chivalric tradition, a game carried on with headlong dash and glorious pageantry, to the accompaniment of music and laughter, and preferably under the gaze of beautiful ladies.

But Stuart's romanticism and his grand style were the lesser part of him; in the end it was his fighting skill that made him great. He was a master of the strategic raid, leading his horsemen behind enemy lines to destroy supplies and communications. His intelligence-gathering was unexcelled; perhaps Robert E Lee's most telling tribute to his general was, 'He never brought me a piece of false information.' With Lee and Jackson, Stuart was part of the triumvirate that time

and again led to victory one of the most remarkable fighting forces ever seen – the Army of Northern Virginia. In short, Jeb Stuart backed up his flash and chivalry with tireless professionalism and hard fighting – until the youthful impetuousness that brought him glory finally became his undoing.

Stuart was born to a large southwestern Virginia family on 6 February 1833; his father was a lawyer and later a Congressman. A disciplined person from childhood, Stuart swore at age of 12 he would never touch alcohol, and kept that vow until the day he died. Taken by the glory of soldiering, he was admitted to the US Military Academy and arrived there in June 1850; on the journey he wrote letters home that already showed the Stuart style – the language is flowery, but also acutely observant.

At West Point Stuart was strong in his studies, but his demerits accumulated spectacularly. That too shows the high-spirited Cavalier the world would know, as does his delight in being dubbed 'Beauty' by his classmates. As a cadet he was already a superb horseman and an incorrigible flirt with the ladies; he filled his spare hours collecting flower specimens and reading Shakespeare, his favorite author.

He graduated 13th in his class of 46 in 1854, having decided to go into mounted service rather than become a 'petty-fogger lawyer' like his father. Soon he was fighting Indians on the frontier with the Mounted Rifles. In 1855 Secretary of War Jefferson Davis created the first two units called Cavalry (as opposed to Dragoons and Mounted Rifles). Stuart was detailed to the First Cavalry in 1855.

That same year he grew his legendary cinnamon-red spade beard and married Flora Cooke, daughter of Dragoon leader Philip St George Cooke. Jeb loved his Flora passionately and apparently remained faithful to her despite many other female claims on his attention. Stuart served in Kansas during the slavery troubles of 1856, was seriously wounded fighting the Cheyenne the next year and was one of Robert E Lee's detail when it captured fanatical abolitionist John Brown at Harper's Ferry in 1859. It was the Brown raid that seemed to light the fuse of war. By the time Jefferson Davis became president of the Confederacy in 1861, Jeb Stuart had already asked him for a commission in the Southern army. He was then 28 years old.

Stuart began the war as an infantry lieutenant but was soon made a captain of cavalry. At the very outset, he displayed his dash in the First Battle of Manassas, leading his men to scatter a force of grandly clad New York Zouaves. He had already come to the attention of another leader on his way to fame, Stonewall Jackson, who admired Stuart's credo: 'If we oppose force to force we cannot win, for their resources are greater than ours. We must substitute *esprit* for numbers. Therefore I strive to inculcate in my men the spirit of the chase.'

Typical uniform and weaponry are displayed in this illustration of a lieutenant in the first Virginia Cavalry Regiment in 1861.

Above: Jefferson Davis and his cabinet meet to review war strategy.

Left. A Currier & Ives print depicts a battle between the Zouaves and the Black Horse Cavalry at Bull Run on 21 July 1861.

In the summer of 1862, Stuart was in Joseph E Johnston's army, preparing to resist General George McClellan and his Army of the Potomac, who were determined to reach Richmond. Stuart's camp was like no other in the army. Frequently the tent echoed with his hearty laughter, and at intervals his banjoist, Sam Sweeney, would enliven the tedium with his tunes. Stuart's field outfit was a bit less gaudy than

his dress uniform, but was still topped by his famous hat with its ostrich plume. He collected a staff known for loyalty, sartorial elegance and professionalism.

Word came in June 1862 that McClellan's army might have an exposed left flank, and Stuart's cavalry were detailed to find out if that were true and to cause a little havoc in Federal communications. Even before he left, Stuart had

After being harassed by Jeb
Stuart's cavalry, Union
General George McClellan
faced Robert E Lee,
Stonewall Jackson and
Stuart in the Seven Days'
Battles.

decided to try the unprecedented stunt of riding right around these 100,000 or so Yankees. He headed out on 12 June 1862, with 1000 troopers, riding north from Richmond. An aide recalled his departure: 'The gray coat buttoned to the chin; the light French saber, the pistol in its black holster; the cavalry boots above the knee, and the brown hat with its black plume floating above the bearded features, the brilliant eyes and the huge moustache, which curled with laughter at the

After being harassed by Jeb
Stuart's cavalry, Union
General George McClellan
faced Robert E Lee,
Stonewall Jackson and
Stuart in the Seven Days'
Battles.

slightest provocation – these made Stuart the perfect picture of a gay cavalier.' An officer shouted, 'When will you be back?' 'It may be years, and it may be forever,' Stuart replied, his laughter fading in the distance.

From Ashland the column turned east to Hanover Court House, where a detail of Yankee cavalry were hurried on their way. At Hawes Shop, on 13 June, the Confederates were confronted by the 5th US Cavalry, who put up a running resistance for awhile but for their trouble had their camp burned by Fitzhugh 'Fitz' Lee.

McClellan, finally realizing that he had a substantial enemy cavalry force in his rear, sent out troopers to run these Rebels aground. Heading this detachment was none other than Philip St George Cooke, Jeb Stuart's father-in-law, who had thrown in his lot with the North. The old Cooke moved slowly; he had spent his life fighting Indians, not relatives.

By then Stuart knew what he needed to know – that the Federal left flank was unsupported, 'in the air' as it was called, across the Chickahominy River. He took his column south, burning bridges and skirmishing as he went, Cooke trailing ineffectually. The Confederates' only close call came on the banks of the Chickahominy; the river was flooded and Cooke was closing in. Stuart detailed men to take planks from local houses and barns and rebuild a burnt bridge. The Rebels crossed and torched the bridge just as the Union riders came into view. Later, one of his staff observed, 'That was a tight place at the river, General. If the enemy had come down on us, you would have been compelled to surrender.' The Cavalier, as he was already known, shot back with a laugh: 'No, one other course was left – to die game.'

Stuart's men arrived back in Richmond on 15 June, having ridden nearly 150 miles, destroyed considerable Union supplies, and made a good haul of prisoners. Confederate casualties totaled one trooper. The raid became the first major element of the Stuart legend. Jeb started the legend himself, reciting for the ladies of Richmond his poem called 'The Ride Around McClellan.'

Soon Johnston attacked McClellan's unsupported column and the Seven Days' Battles were on. At the end of that week Johnston was a casualty and the new commander was Robert E Lee, who renamed his forces the Army of Northern Virginia and made Jeb Stuart a major general in charge of the army's cavalry. Now the triumvirate was ready for action: Lee the tactician, Jackson the strong right arm, Stuart the eyes and ears of the army.

McClellan was not really beaten during the Seven Days, but nonetheless he sailed his army back to Washington. Then the focus of Union efforts in the East shifted to the Federal Army of the Potomac, which was commanded by a blowhard general named John Pope.

Pope sent two brigades of cavalry Stuart's way

in mid-August 1862. They accomplished little, but in one raid at Verdiersville did capture a symbolic prize – The Cavalier's plumed hat. This was not the sort of insult to be countenanced from Yankees. Jeb got permission for a raid on Union railroads and rode out on 22 August saying, 'I'm going after my hat.'

With 1500 sabers and two guns, Stuart crossed the Rappahannock and entered Warrenton without seeing a Yankee. The night of the 22nd found them near Catlett's Station, where the Federals were encamped in a driving rainstorm. A Union officer, an old friend of Jeb's from Indian-fighting days, had just raised a glass and proclaimed to his fellows, 'This is something like comfort. I hope Jeb Stuart won't disturb us tonight.' Suddenly, above the rain, came the clamor of bugles and the spine-chilling Rebel yell. The Federal officer banged his fist on the table, crying, 'There he is, by God!'

As the Confederates poured into the camp, the bluecoats scattered in all directions, some getting entangled in their tents and finding themselves sabered from the outside. Hampered as they were in the rain, however, the Confederates were unable to hang on to their prisoners, and the railroad bridge refused to burn. Still, they made away with most of the camp's supplies. In Warrenton next day Stuart took stock of his haul; besides general materiél, it included a number of General

Left: Novelist John E Cooke, who was a cousin of Jeb Stuart's wife Flora, travelled with Stuart throughout the war, keeping diaries for the memoirs he later wrote.

Below: Night amusements around the Confederate camp fire.

An engraving depicts the uniform of the Maryland Guard.

An engraving of a Confederate troop titled *Route Step*.

Pope's staff, a good deal of money, and the general's papers, baggage, and, most appropriately, his dress coat. Directly Stuart sent a dispatch to Pope: 'General: You have my hat and plume. I have your best coat. I have the honor to propose a cartel for a fair exchange of the prisoners.'

The Catlett's Station raid helped to position Lee's troops for the ensuing rout of Pope at Second Manassas. In his report Stuart claimed the raid had 'inflicted a mortifying disaster upon the general himself in the loss of his personal baggage.' Lee noted dryly to Richmond, 'The General deals in the flowery style.' Privately, Jeb gleefully wrote to Flora, 'I have had my revenge out of Pope.'

Over the summer of 1862, Lee had stymied McClellan and thrashed Pope. Now he looked for new fields to conquer, and his thoughts moved north, into enemy territory – Maryland, where food and supplies were in abundance, and there were a good many Confederate sympathizers who might sign up with the South. On 4 September, with Stuart's cavalry patrolling the rear, the Army of Northern Virginia crossed the Potomac into Maryland on an invasion of the North.

As usual, Jeb did not let the exigencies of war interfere with his social life. One evening during the Maryland campaign found him at a ball he had organized in Urbana, dancing with the local belles, when word came of Yankee cavalry in the Southern camps. The music stuttered to a halt as the Confederate officers leapt to their horses. Soon the enemy had been sent running and The Cavalier and his staff were back and ready to resume dancing.

A few days later Stuart was helping Jackson take Harper's Ferry while Lee shadowed the slow-moving Army of the Potomac. But Lee seemed to stumble every time he entered enemy soil. Marylanders were unco-operative, and, far worse, a copy of Lee's disposition order was found in a field by a Federal soldier. Now McClellan had all the information he needed to smash Lee. But on 14 August Lee held his line by a thread at Antietam Creek in the bloodiest day's fighting of the war. The result was a stalemate, but Lee's invasion was ended, and the North was content to call Antietam a victory, if a dubious one.

For a month Stuart and his entourage rested at The Bower, a plantation near Martinsburg in West Virginia. The time was spent flirting, dancing, serenading the ladies, and planning for the campaigns to come. From miles around people came to see and revel with the cavalrymen, enchanted by their gallantry, captivated by stories of their exploits, and buoyed up by their irrepressible gaiety amid the fears and privations of war.

In October new orders arrived: there was to be a raid into Pennsylvania to capture the town of Chambersburg. On the 9th, 1800 troopers pulled out, from the brigades of Fitz Lee, Wade Hampton, and 'Grumble' Jones. Also on the ride was a

23-year-old gunner named John Pelham. Tall, graceful, outlandishly handsome, and a legendary wooer of young ladies, Pelham was one of the bravest and best artillerists of the war. Stuart loved him like a son and made Pelham head of his horse artillery.

The column headed north for the Pennsylvania line, as usual, brushing aside parties of Federal cavalry. Passing Mercersburg, they turned east while Union telegraph wires hummed with the report that Stuart was up to his tricks again. By the evening of the 9th, despite torrents of rain, the Rebel riders were in Chambersburg demanding a quick surrender. The citizens were happy to oblige. Before going to sleep they had stores and supplies to commandeer or destroy; particularly welcome was an abundance of uniforms, which the ragged Confederates did not scorn for being blue. At daybreak on the 10th, the column was off again, winding south. Meanwhile McClellan had geared up most of his cavalry to head off the 'retreat' of these Rebels; apparently he did not suspect that Stuart was going to circle him again.

The Cavalier kept his men riding steadily, knowing he had no time to spare. As the hours wore on, the men dozed in the saddle, the horses stumbling down the road. Incredibly, at night Stuart detoured for an hour to visit a lady acquaintance in Urbana. Finally, on the 12th, the column arrived at a ford on the Potomac just as the Federal advance reached them. Stuart roused his men to a charge and chased the Federal advance for a mile. John Pelham and William H F 'Rooney' Lee, Robert E Lee's son, arrived and began firing away at the growing number of Yankees near the river. The chance of the Southerners getting across to safety seemed very slim, until Rooney tried a trick worthy of Jeb himself: he sent a note to the Federal commander demanding surrender and saying Stuart was at hand with a large force. The Federals fled.

On 12 October Stuart's Chambersburg Raid ended at Leesburg. He and his men had covered 126 miles in four days, the last 24 hours riding 80 miles without a halt. They had commandeered 1200 horses, outwitted the whole Yankee cavalry, circled McClellan again, and lost only three men. It had been one of The Cavalier's most spectacular outings.

Hearing of the raid, Lincoln observed, 'When I was a boy we used to play a game – three times around, and out. Stuart has been around McClellan twice. If he goes around him once more, gentlemen, McClellan will be out.'

In fact, Lincoln did not wait for the third time; on 5 November he removed McClellan from command of the Army of the Potomac and appointed Ambrose Burnside in his stead. Burnside happened to be one of the most inept generals of all time, and soon proved it at Fredericksburg, where, on 13 December 1862, he threw his whole army at Lee's position and lost 13,000 casualties to the South's 5000.

Above: The Confederate dead after Antietam.

The rebels covered by a ledge of rock

Left: An artist's depiction of a Confederate line at Sharpsburg, or Antietam.

Troops bid farewell as General George McClellan takes leave of his army on 10 November 1862.

After that debacle for the North, Lee sent Stuart's cavalry on a series of raids against Burnside's communications. The last and most elaborate of these was the Dumfries Raid that pulled out of Fredericksburg on 26 December 1862, with 1800 men and four guns under John Pelham. They crossed the Rappahannock and headed east, toward the lines of supply that flowed out of Washington to the Army of the Potomac.

At Morrisville Stuart broke his column into three brigades under Rooney Lee, Wade Hampton and Fitz Lee. After a day of raiding, Rooney Lee and Stuart attacked the Federal garrison at Dumfries. When the Yankees there proved too strong to be budged, Stuart decided to try his luck north of the Rappahannock. There was skirmishing throughout the 28th, with a good haul of prisoners and supplies. At Occoquan Federal camps were overrun and the three columns reunited.

After dark the Confederates captured a Union telegraph office at Burke's Station, and Stuart could not resist razzing the authorities in Washington. After listening in on notices from Washington about operations to catch him, Jeb sent a telegram of his own to the quartermaster-general of the Union army: 'Quality of the mules lately furnished me very poor. Interferes seriously with movement of captured wagons. JEB Stuart.' On 31 December the raiders returned to Confederate lines at Culpeper with 200 prisoners, the

same number of horses, 20 enemy wagons and teams, and a wagonload of weapons. Losses had been one killed, 13 wounded, 13 missing.

As 1863 began, Southern fortunes had never been more hopeful in the Eastern Theater of the war, the spirit of the soldiers never more exultant after having stymied or whipped the enormous and well-outfitted Army of the Potomac three times in a row. The triumvirate of Lee, Jackson and Stuart was about to send those spirits still higher before the zenith was reached.

By the beginning of the year, most Rebel cavalrymen had been equipped with breech-loading single-shot carbines and repeating pistols, a considerable improvement over the awkward infantry muzzle-loaders and single-shot horse pistols with which they had begun the war. But the new year also brought an ominous new aggressiveness from the Yankee cavalry. In March 3000 Union cavalrymen nearly swamped Fitz Lee near Culpeper. Among the dead was the irreplaceable gunner John Pelham, a legend at age 23. The man who brought the news to Stuart wrote, 'I shall never forget his look of distress and horror.' Soon enough The Cavalier would be laughing again, but that laughter would ring increasingly hollow over the next months.

In January Lincoln replaced the hapless Ambrose Burnside with 'Fighting Joe' Hooker, who revitalized the Army of the Potomac and proclaimed, 'God have mercy on General Lee, for

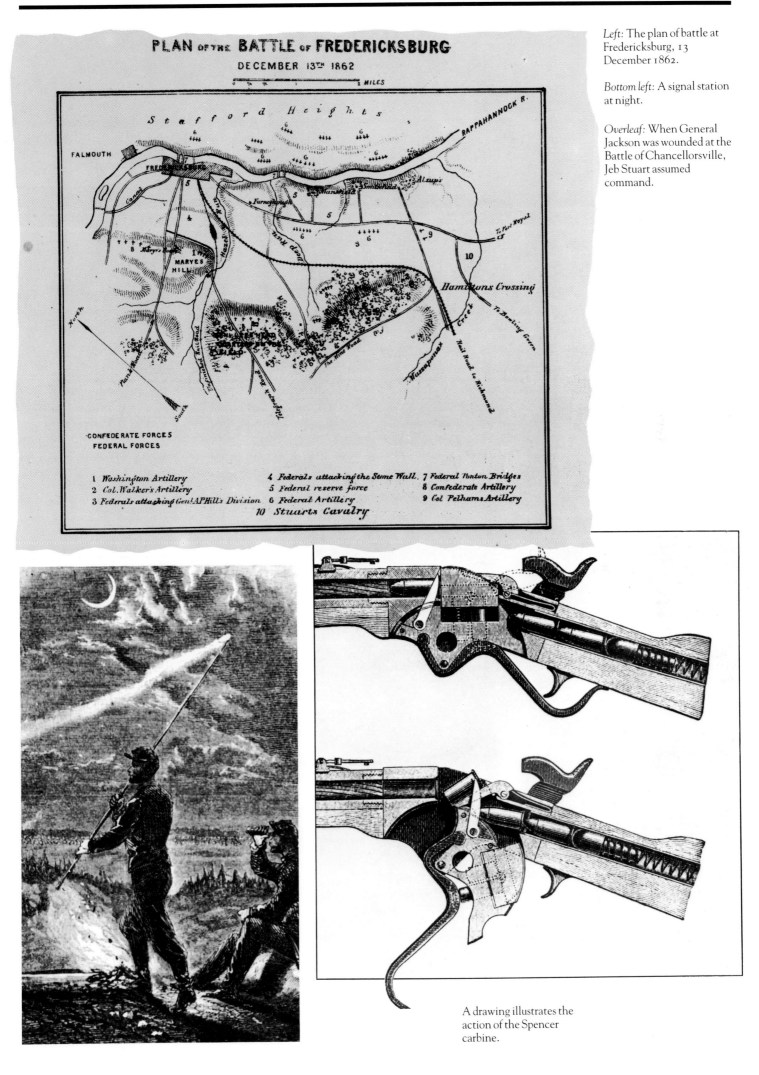

PLAN OF THE **BATTLE** OF **FREDERICKSBURG**

DECEMBER 13TH 1862

2 MILES

S t a f f o r d   H e i g h t s

RAPPAHANNOCK R.

FALMOUTH

FREDERICKSBURG

MARYES HILL

Hamiltons Crossing

North

South

To Port Royal

To Bowling Green

Rail Road to Richmond

CONFEDERATE FORCES
FEDERAL FORCES

1 *Washington Artillery*
2 *Col. Walker's Artillery*
3 *Federals attacking Gen! AP Hill's Division*

4 *Federals attacking the Stone Wall.*
5 *Federal reserve force*
6 *Federal Artillery*

7 *Federal Ponton Bridges*
8 *Confederate Artillery*
9 *Col Pelham's Artillery*

10 *Stuarts Cavalry*

Left: The plan of battle at Fredericksburg, 13 December 1862.

Bottom left: A signal station at night.

Overleaf: When General Jackson was wounded at the Battle of Chancellorsville, Jeb Stuart assumed command.

A drawing illustrates the action of the Spencer carbine.

GEN. HOOKER'S HEAD QUARTE

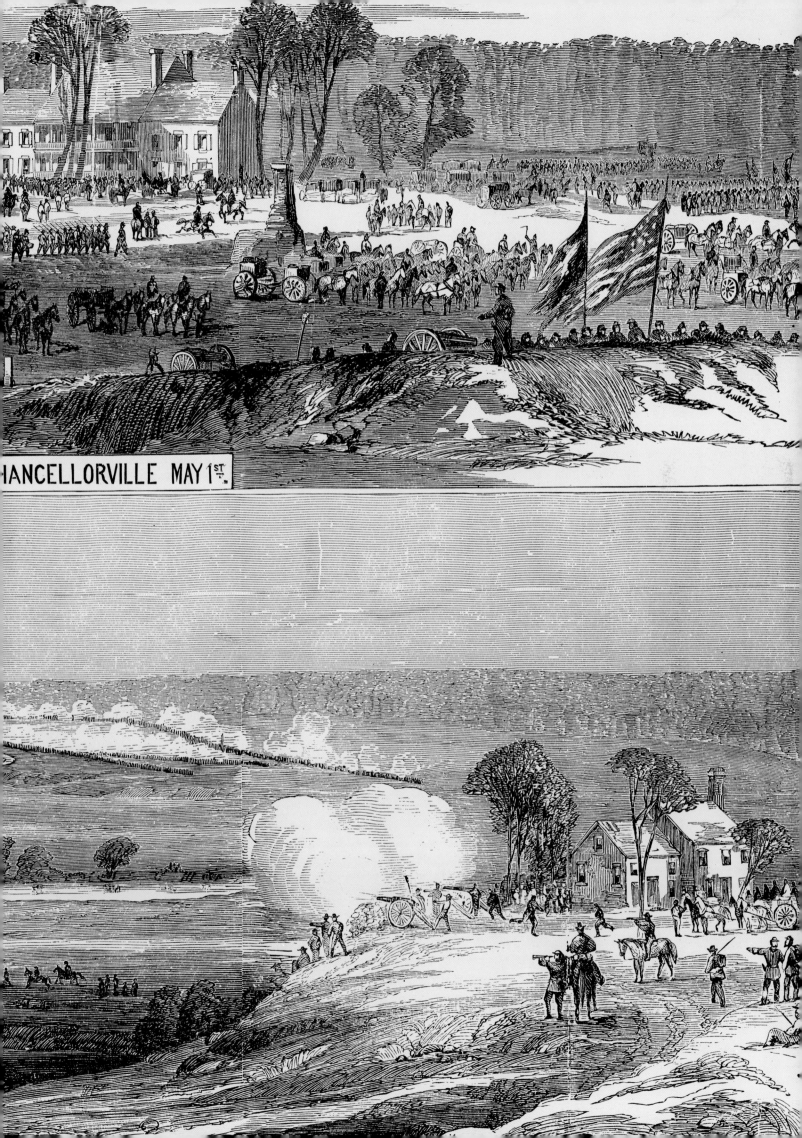

CHANCELLORVILLE MAY 1ST.

I will not.' Hooker developed a plan for holding Lee in position at Fredericksburg with a detachment while swinging the rest of his army around to come in behind the Confederates. In late April 1863 Hooker put his army in motion into Virginia. Shadowing the enemy move was Stuart's cavalry; before long Stuart had informed Lee of Hooker's little game, and Lee made his preparations.

On 31 April Hooker, moving his forces towards Lee's rear, was surprised to find Confederates waiting for him near a little clearing called Chancellorsville. Hooker could have brushed them away easily; instead, he lost his nerve, pulling back into the dense forest of the Wilderness. Soon Stuart had discovered that the enemy right flank was in the air. Lee and Jackson made their plans that night, and next day Jackson marched his men around and routed that right flank.

The result was Lee's greatest victory. But in the confusion of that night Confederate fortunes began to change once and for all: Stonewall Jackson was wounded accidentally by his own men and out of the battle (forever, as it turned out, for he died eight days later). Next day Stuart was given command of Jackson's forces, and in the only infantry command of his life drove his men right to the Federal headquarters at Chancellorsville, showing the same brilliance and dash he did with his cavalry.

After Chancellorsville there was talk of Stuart being given Jackson's command permanently, but Stuart did not ask for it, and Lee wisely left him where he was. As a Confederate officer wrote, 'Some men are born to write great works, others to paint great pictures, others to rule over nations. Stuart was born to fight cavalry.'

Once again Lee could not restrain himself from thinking about what he could accomplish by invading the North. The safer and, as it turned out, wiser course would have been to stay put and fight a defensive war. But Lee was, above all, aggressive, and after Chancellorsville, where he had beaten an army nearly twice his size, it seemed his men could do anything. Thus he made the most fateful decision of his career – to march into Pennsylvania on a second invasion of the North.

In the first week of June 1863 Lee concentrated at Culpeper, preparing to send his forces through Maryland into Pennsylvania. Meanwhile Joe Hooker sent 11,000 cavalrymen under General Alfred Pleasonton to scout the new Rebel movement. In the early morning of 9 June Stuart's cavalry lay along the Rappahannock in the vicinity of Brandy Station, screening Lee's army.

At four in the morning a Southern guard suddenly screamed, 'Yankees! Great God, millions of 'em!' Two columns of Federal cavalry over 10,000 men, smashed into Stuart's camps, one column near Beverly Ford and the other six miles to the south at Kelly's Ford. For once the Yankees

Fierce fighting between cavalry forces at Chancellorsville.

had caught The Cavalier napping, and their initial assault was devastating. The Southern camps erupted in fire and chaos, the men struggling to mount their nervous horses. Barefoot and hatless on his horse, 'Grumble' Jones quickly got his men into the fray, only to find himself pushed back toward Brandy Station. To the south, Pleasonton's attack made less headway against Wade Hampton and Beverly Robertson.

Soon Stuart was getting the reports, but they seemed unbelievable. This was not the Yankee cavalry that he knew. Hearing that Federals were approaching the rear of his headquarters, Stuart sent a rider to 'see what all this foolishness is about.' Soon he could hear enemy cannon in his rear. He ordered his nearest regiments to secure Fleetwood Hill, the key position in the area. Thousands of riders wheeled toward the hill. An observer recalled, 'It was a thrilling sight to see these dashing horsemen draw their sabers and start for the hill at a gallop. The lines met on the hill. It was like what we read of in the days of chivalry, acres and acres of horsemen sparkling with sabers . . . flags above them, hurled against each other at full speed and meeting with a shock that made the earth tremble.'

Though the infantry was on the field around Brandy Station, the battle was largely a cavalry affair – the largest mounted engagement of the war. Moreover, in the fighting that raged all day up and down the river, most of the action was pursued with sabers; for one of the only times in the war, there was comparatively little shooting to be heard. A participant remembered the style of the fighting: 'Two fellows put at me. The first one fired at me and missed. Before he could again

Above: Charge of the 6th New York Cavalry at Brandy Station.

Left: Brigadier General Wade Hampton, whose charge helped secure the Confederate position on Fleetwood Hill at Brandy Station, was wounded three times during the war.

cock his revolver I succeeded in closing with him. My saber took him just in the neck, and must have cut the jugular. The blood gushed out in a black-looking stream; he gave a horrible yell.'

Convinced, finally, that he was in trouble, Stuart began to regroup his forces. Fleetwood Hill changed hands several times, thousands of horses roaring back and forth in the melée, before a determined charge by Wade Hampton secured the position and the spirit and experience of the Southern troopers began to prevail. But not until dark, after a full day of fighting, did the Federals pull away to the east.

The South had suffered 523 casualties, the North 936, over half of them captured. Jeb Stuart had won the field at the battle of Brandy Station, but it was an uneasy victory. The new confidence of the Union cavalry was evident to all. A Southern officer later wrote, 'One result of incalculable importance certainly did follow this battle . . . it *made* the Federal cavalry. Up to that time confessedly inferior to the Southern horsemen, they gained on this day that confidence in themselves and in their commanders which enabled them to contest so fiercely the subsequent battlefields.' Moreover, now Joe Hooker knew that Lee was heading north, and readied his army to shadow Lee's every move.

Suddenly The Cavalier found his bright star tarnished. The Richmond papers excoriated him in their usual vitriolic terms: '. . . this puffed up cavalry – has been twice, if not three times, surprised since the battles of December, and such repeated accidents can be regarded as nothing but the necessary consequences of negligence and bad management.' This editor went on to say that 'a few vain and weak-headed officers' seemed to find the war a 'tournament, invented and supported for [their] pleasure.'

This was more serious stuff than losing a hat. Stuart brooded, looking for his chance at revenge. In the first week of June, he mounted a grand cavalry review, parading his 12,000 men and 24 guns twice, once for his staff and again for General Lee. It was the peak of their size and strength, and of their pride as well.

As Lee moved into Pennsylvania, Federal cavalry hounded the far-flung Confederate forces, fighting a running series of skirmishes that kept Stuart and Lee blind as to the position and strength of the Union army. Finally Stuart proposed a plan, one that would locate the enemy and, in the process, perhaps reclaim his glory: his men would once again ride around the Army of the Potomac. In an ambiguously worded order, Lee seemed to give Stuart free rein. On 24 June 1863 the troopers set out on what seemed like another good bit of fun.

But as had happened in Maryland the last time that Lee stepped into enemy territory, little seemed to go right for the South. Stuart began his raid in usual form, striking the Federal supply line at Rockville and capturing 125 wagons and many prisoners. As he continued on, however, the captured wagons and bluecoats slowed him down. Furthermore, he found the Army of the Potomac much more widely disposed than expected, and he had to detour farther and farther east to get around them. At Westminster, Maryland, on 29 June, a large body of Federal cavalry charged Stuart's men. These were driven off, but the next day at Hanover, Pennsylvania, there was a close call. Finding enemy riders in Hanover, a detachment of Confederates attacked and drove them out. But then the Northerners mounted a spirited countercharge, and from their windows citizens pelted the Rebels with muskets and shotguns.

James Ewell Brown Stuart was a promising captain in the US Army when he joined the Confederate army in 1861, becoming a lieutenant colonel to begin his illustrious career with the 1st Virginia Cavalry.

Stuart arrived and tried to rally his men; instead, he was taken up in the flight just in front of the Federal pursuit.

With a laugh, Stuart drew his saber and shouted to one of his staff: 'rally them, Blackford!' It was a joke; perhaps he meant the enemy. Jumping a hedge at the roadside, Stuart and William Blackford pounded off across a field with Yankee bullets singing around them. Suddenly a 15-foot ditch appeared in their path. Without hesitation both men spurred their horses on, sailing into the air. Blackford later recalled, 'I shall never forget the glimpse I then saw of this beautiful animal away up in midair over the chasm and Stuart's fine figure sitting erect and firm in the saddle.' They made the ditch with room to spare, and were away with the men.

That instant when the laughing Stuart was poised in midair, in enemy territory amid a spray of bullets, might stand for his last lightning flash of glory. For The Cavalier, for his troopers, for the South, it was to be downhill riding from that time forward.

In the end Stuart's last ride around the enemy came to little good and was responsible for what ended as a catastrophe: it deprived Lee's army of their eyes and ears just when they needed them most. Marching blind into enemy territory, the Confederate infantry stumbled over the Federals in a little town called Gettysburg, and the greatest battle to take place on the North American continent erupted in the July heat. Stuart rejoined the army on the second day of battle, 2 July, and did no fighting until the next day. Then The Cavalier tried and failed to take his cavalry around the Union right while Pickett's charge was turned back by the middle of the Federal line. Southern fortunes had crested and were never to rise again.

Finally, the Army of Northern Virginia headed south in unmitigated defeat for the first time. There would be a good deal more riding and fighting for Jeb Stuart and his men, and he was never to lose his spirit or his faith in the cause.

For The Cavalier the road ended on 11 May 1864 at Yellow Tavern, Virginia, in fighting with Sheridan, a misfit whom the Civil War elevated to a general in the Union army and who turned into the most ferocious cavalryman on either side. The first bullet to touch Jeb Stuart in the war was sufficient; he went down as he had more than once prophesied, in the saddle in the middle of the fighting, a rose in his lapel. As he was placed in the ambulance, he rose to shout, 'Go back! Do your duty as I've done mine. I would rather die than be whipped!' But now Phil Sheridan was calling the shots.

On his deathbed, Jeb was persuaded to break his childhood vow and take a swallow of spirits. It could not halt the inevitable. He died on 12 May, aged 32, already a legend. With him died, once and for all, the old romantic myth of the cavalryman. The future belonged to the plain hard fighters like Phil Sheridan.

Left: The Battle at Yellow Tavern, Virginia, on 11 May 1864, where Jeb Stuart was mortally wounded after he had emptied his pistol firing at the Union Cavalry.

Below: A scene from the battle at Gettysburg.

Robert E Lee

Chancellorsville

The Battle of Chancellorsville, 1-4 May, 1863.

Above: A typical Confederate sailor's uniform.

By late May 1862, the Civil War had been underway for thirteen months. Hostilities had reached a stalemate – temporary, but for the moment neither side could claim any decisive military advantage. The Confederate forces had won several battles: Manassas (or Bull Run), and at McDowell and Front Royal, as part of Jackson's Shenandoah Valley Campaign. The Federal forces could point to such victories as the capture of New Orleans and Forts Henry and Donelson. However, most of the major engagements were inconclusive, like the naval battle between the *Monitor* and the *Merrimac* or the Battle of Shiloh.

Another point now clear was that the war was not going to end quickly, as both sides had been hoping. Consciously or otherwise, neither the Federal nor the Confederate leaders truly wanted to undertake a major war, one that would pit massive military forces against one another over vast regions while killing great numbers of civilians as well as military personnel and destroying incalculabale amounts of property and matériel. Yet after thirteen months, both sides were wandering deeper into just that quagmire. And no end was in sight.

Frustration would probably be the word that best summed up the situations and feelings of all Americans in late May 1862, and no one felt that frustration more than Robert E Lee. Even his position in the Confederate Army was one of frustrating ambiguity: he held the rank of full general and since March had been formally assigned by Jefferson Davis, President of the Confederate States, to oversee 'the conduct of military operations in the armies of the Confederacy,' but Lee had learned from his first year's service under Davis just how maddeningly restricted his actual authority was. On one side he was overruled by Jefferson Davis himself, touchy about his own position to the point of neuroticism and determined to prove his military credentials; on

the other side, Lee was constantly upstaged by the various prima donnas serving as Confederate generals, all determined to claim the privileges of rank and command. Only a man as innately confident in himself as Lee was, and as endowed with tact and diplomacy, could have held on during these thirteen months.

What made his situation even more incredible is that this was the very man who had initially been asked by President Abraham Lincoln (through an intermediary) to command the Federal army about to be organized to bring the seceding Confederate states back into line. That was on 18 April 1861. Lee declined the offer courteously, and with sadness too. Early that year, writing from Texas of secession, he had said: 'As an American citizen I take great pride in my country. . . . I can anticipate no greater calamity for this country than a dissolution of the Union. It would be an accumulation of all the evils we complain of.' As for slavery, he had already written, 'There are few, I believe, but will acknowledge that slavery as an institution is a moral and political evil.' He had set free the slaves he owned in his own right by inheritance and was 'in favor of freeing all slaves in the South.' On the other hand, he felt he 'could take no part in an invasion of the Southern States.' In particular, he could not, by all he had been taught and held dear, take part in an invasion of his native state of Virginia. His gallant father, Henry 'Light-Horse Harry' Lee, who had not only distinguished himself as a soldier in the Revolutionary War but had heartily advocated the ratification of the Constitution of the United States, had once said in debate: 'Virginia is my country; her I will obey, however lamentable the fate to which it may subject me.' Such was the heritage in which Robert E Lee was reared; such was his first loyalty.

On 22 April Lee accepted the command of his state's military forces offered to him by the governor, John Letcher. And when Virginia formally joined the Confederacy on 24 April, Lee did not concern himself for a moment with the fact that as a major general he was going to have to cede authority often to men who held only the rank of brigadier general in the Confederate Army. All Lee cared about was defending Virginia from imminent invasion by Federal forces.

Virginian forces had immediately seized the two most valuable Federal installations in the state – the rifle-producing armory at Harper's Ferry and the naval yard at Norfolk. (What they did not take was the formidable Fort Monroe, opposite Norfolk, which would remain in Federal hands throughout the war and prove to be a continuing threat, providing as it did access to the Peninsula.) On 10 May 1861 President Davis formally put Lee in charge of all Confederate troops in Virginia, for units from other states were now appearing. Lee's actual responsibilities, however, were still restricted to preparing troops for combat: in actual engagements with the Federals, the troops were to be commanded by

Below: An etching depicts Robert E Lee and Thomas J Jackson in council behind the line of battle.

W. L. Sheppard

Above: W L Sheppard's illustration of the Confederate line awaiting orders in the Wilderness.

Left: The aftermath of Sedgwick's assault, 3 May 1863, on Marye's Heights. Pictured are Confederate caisson wagons and horses, destroyed by a shot from the Federal siege-gun battery.

other Confederate generals. It was one of several anomalies that would plague the Confederacy that during these crucial first months of the war Robert E Lee was reduced to functioning pretty much as a quartermaster, organizing subsistence, arms, and transport for the troops, and as a desk-bound administrator.

Finally, on 28 July 1861, Lee was allowed to go off to the mountainous region of northwestern Virginia, where Virginians themselves were proving to be unsympathetic to joining in the Confederate cause and where Union forces were expected soon to appear. Yet Lee's role was still to be little more than a 'troubleshooter' and co-ordinator; he lacked full command authority should combat ensue. Although he worked marvels in getting the disorganized forces into shape and in obtaining some co-operation among three Confederate generals there – W W Loring, Henry Wise and John Floyd – in the end Lee could not exert much influence on events in this region. His one great chance came at Cheat Mountain (in what would soon become West Virginia), from 10-15 September 1861, a campaign he planned. Lee had hoped to catch the Federal forces on the mountain by surprise, but rain and poor co-ordination among the officers in the field left the inexperienced Confederate forces so exposed that Lee had to abandon his plan and the field. While not a major defeat – perhaps 120 Confederates killed, wounded, or captured – it was a considerable blow to Lee's reputation. He was, characteristically, undisturbed when one of his officers, General William E Stark, told him that the press was denouncing him, people losing confidence in him, that the army had needed a victory to instill it with enthusiasm. Unruffled, he replied with a smile: 'I could not afford to sacrifice the lives of five or six hundred of my people to silence public clamor.'

Lee returned to Richmond, the Confederate capital, on 31 October 1861, and was asked by President Davis to undertake yet another organizational task: building up the defenses along the coasts of South Carolina and Georgia to resist bombardments from Federal ships and hold off any possible invasion forces. He succeeded so admirably that he rendered the coast cities of those two states impregnable against all assaults by sea. Still, it was hardly the kind of chore, however vital to the Confederacy, to gain him public acclaim. Even some of his fellow Virginians took to calling him by the condescending name 'Granny' – 'too tender to shed blood' was implied and at times openly expressed. Again, having achieved what he had been sent to do, Lee returned to Richmond and resumed his post there without a word of complaint or any sign that he was displeased by his situation or the talk about

A Confederate 150-pounder Armstrong breech-loading rifled cannon at Fort Fisher, near Wilmington.

Opposite: General Robert E Lee became commander in chief of the Confederate forces two days after resigning his commission in the US Army. Despite his rank, Lee usually wore the uniform of a Confederate colonel.

town. It was at this point that Davis subjected him to the ultimate frustration, putting him in charge of 'the conduct of military operations in the armies of the Confederacy' yet allowing him no true authority to impose a grand strategy or to direct campaigns.

In the ensuing months, Lee's frustration only intensified as he had to sit in Richmond, shuffling papers and attending to Davis while the Confederate forces in the field yielded more and more of northern Virginia to the Federals. In particular, General Joseph E Johnston had adopted a strategy that Lee found totally opposite to his own preferred one of taking the offensive: Johnston advocated withdrawing to a perimeter around Richmond. And because Johnston essentially went his own way, by mid-May 1862 that was in fact what had happened. To the northwest the Confederate forces had been pulled back from the Manassas line, while to the southeast Yorktown and the invaluable Norfolk Navy Yard had been abandoned (with the result, too, that the symbolic *Merrimac*, or *Virginia* as the Confederates called it, had been scuttled). And on 14 May Lee was called to an emergency meeting at which he heard President Davis and his cabinet actually discussing what might have to be done if Richmond were abandoned. At that Lee burst forth with a passion he seldom revealed: 'But Richmond must be defended!'

In the days following the momentous meeting Lee remained virtually powerless to stop General Johnston's continuing withdrawal of Confederate

forces closer and closer to Richmond. Finally, though, Johnston decided to engage the Federals at a point only about 10 miles due east of the capital, just south of the Chickahominy River along a battle line running from Fair Oaks, a station on the York River Railroad, to Seven Pines, a junction of the Williamsburg and Nine Mile Roads. Johnston still refused to inform Lee or Davis about his specific plans, but on 31 May Johnston's forces attacked the Federal forces under the command of General George McClellan. The resulting battle was one of almost total confusion and errors, in part due to the boggy terrain and muddy roads, in part to Johnston's refusal to provide clear communications. When Lee and Davis rode out from Richmond in the afternoon, Johnston essentially ignored them. By the end of the afternoon, however, he could no longer avoid them: he was seriously wounded and had to be carried into their presence before being taken off to Richmond. As night fell both sides simply stopped fighting. Lee and Davis rode their horses back to Richmond through the chaos of men and animals and vehicles that were trying to deal with the thousands of Confederate casualties. Finally President Jefferson Davis turned to Robert E Lee and appointed him to command the Confederate army in Virginia. It had been over 13 months since Lee had accepted a post with the seceding state of Virginia – and Appomattox was only some 34 months in the future.

The formal letter of appointment came on 1 June 1862, and Lee immediately set off to direct

Below: A Currier & Ives print depicting the Battle of Fair Oaks, Virginia, 31 May 1862.

General Winfield Scott (1786-1866) praised Robert E Lee after his service in Mexico. After a distinguished military career, Scott retired from his position as general in chief of the US Army in 1861, at the age of 75.

the battle that had been renewed at Seven Pines that morning. He found the situation so unpromising that he ordered the Confederate forces to withdraw to the positions they had occupied before the battle began. Hardly the most auspicious beginning for a new commander, but Lee really had no choice. Casualties had been heavy (over 6000 for the Confederates, over 5000 for the Federals), and in any case, the point had been made: the Confederate army had finally taken the offensive against the Federal forces advancing on Richmond and although it could hardly claim victory, the Federals had been stopped. What Lee needed for the moment was time to regroup, to institute his own strategy and tactics, to instill a new spirit into the Confederate troops in what he now designated the Army of Northern Virginia.

He also had to win over his own fellow Confederate generals and officers, many of whom were doubtful that Lee was the man to replace Johnston. Few were really aware of what Lee had been contributing to the Confederate cause during the first fourteen months. Considering what Lee's reputation would be within one month from his appointment, it is hard to believe that he was still far from the idol of the Confederacy.

Among Virginians Lee had, of course, a measure of distinction because of the magic aura of his name and the illustrious families to which he was

related by direct descent or marriage – the Washingtons, Curtises, Randolphs, Carters. Was it not his own father, the dashing 'Light Horse Harry' Lee, who had coined that phrase forever evoking the image of the Father of his country: 'First in war, first in peace, and first in the hearts of his countrymen'? Indeed, Robert E Lee spent his boyhood in Alexandria, a town redolent of the memory of George Washington. He worshipped in the same church in which Washington had been a pew-holder. This early influence undoubtedly had much to do with molding the man he became – calm, dignified, a true soldier, for whom duty was, as he once expressed it, 'the sublimest word in our language.' His father died when he was only 11, and although he had older brothers, and sisters too, it was he who selflessly cared for his invalid mother with a rare devotion. After he had left for West Point she wrote him: 'You have been both son and daughter to me.'

At West Point, which he entered in 1825 when he was 18, his record, both in his studies and in his conduct, was exemplary. He graduated second in his class of 46, and without a single demerit throughout his entire four years as a cadet. By his classmates, many of whom he was to serve with or fight against in the Civil War, he was admired and loved. One of them, Joseph E Johnston, with whom he was particularly close, wrote of him in that period: 'We had the same intimate associates, who thought as I did, that no other youth or man so united the qualities that win warm friendship and command high respect.' Upon graduation he was appointed corps adjutant with the Engineers, that corps from which came nearly all the officers who attained high rank during the war. During the next 17 years Lee carried out a series of assignments typical of a career officer of that era – with a few notable exceptions.

Like other West Pointers who were later to figure prominently in the Civil War, he first won his military spurs, and glory, in the Mexican War. General-in-Chief of the US Army Winfield Scott had become aware of Lee's strengths and in January 1847 personally asked to have him transferred to his headquarters staff. Lee went ashore at Vera Cruz in March 1847, and from then until the American forces entered Mexico City in triumph on 14 September distinguished himself on numerous occasions by both his intelligent reconnaissance and his physical courage. When the war in Mexico ended, Lee was brevetted to the rank of full colonel: most important, he had gained an enviable reputation among all who served in Mexico, particularly General Scott, who declared of him afterward that he was the very best soldier he ever saw in the field.

Returning to the routine of a career officer, Lee's only regret about his chosen profession was the frequent prolonged absences from home it demanded. In 1831 he had married Mary Anne Randolph Custis, a great-granddaughter of Martha Washington, toward whom he showed

Above: An illustration of the last meeting between General Scott and the Cabinet, as it appeared in *Harper's Weekly*.

the same caring devotion as he had toward his mother. With the seven children eventually born to them, he cherished family life in the stately residence at Arlington given to his wife by her father. (Upon the outbreak of the Civil War they had to leave Arlington House, which was taken over as headquarters for the Union army. After the war it was confiscated for nonpayment of taxes and established as a national memorial.)

Again for a time Lee attained some prominence, in military circles at least, when in 1852-5 he served as superintendent of West Point. And yet once more, in 1859, he had another brush with history when he commanded the troops sent to Harper's Ferry to put down the insurrectionists led by a man Washington viewed as a dangerous fanatic, John Brown. Interestingly, Lee's aide on that occasion was J E B Stuart.

Above: A sketch by Porte Crayon from *Harper's Weekly* titled *En Route for Harper's Ferry.* Lee commanded the Federal troops sent to Harper's Ferry to put down the raid led by John Brown, in October 1859.

Obviously, then, Lee did have a fine reputation as a military man. Has there been any other individual in all history who was offered the command of both great *opposing* armies in a war? But this Lee would have considered irrelevant as he began to map his campaign early in June 1862. His immediate goal, as he wrote to President Davis, was 'to drive our enemies back to their homes' and thus 'change the character of the war.' By that Lee meant to make the North realize that it would be futile to pursue the South on the battlefield. His strategy would be to seize the initiative, to take the offensive, to become an army that acted rather than reacted, one that moved and maneuvered. He knew he could count on such officers as Jeb Stuart and Stonewall Jackson to support him in this new approach, and he figured he would win over his other generals and their men.

To that end Lee immediately set out to re-organize and revitalize the Army of Northern Virginia. Setting up his headquarters in Dabbs House, east of the Richmond city limits, Lee soon let all his men know that he was in charge. He selected his own staff officers, tightened up the organization, and generally instilled a new sense of order and purpose in his troops. As one officer expressed it: there was 'the new impulse from Lee's headquarters . . . the network of a general organization was cast over the whole army.' And unlike General Johnston and so many other commanders (on both sides), Lee truly believed in communicating, in co-operation, in consideration. All those years of routine assignments at remote outpost and forts, all those years of observing how fellow officers behaved, had not been lost on Robert E Lee. The years of frustration were now to pay off in this supremely able and confident commander.

After barely three weeks Lee felt he was ready to take the offensive, and on 23 June he called his four top generals – Jackson, Longstreet, D H Hill, and A P Hill – to co-ordinate his plans. General George McClellan still threatened Richmond with his greatly superior numbers and weaponry; the Federals were within six miles of the city limits. But Lee also knew that McClellan was an extremely methodical and cautious commander, one who might be thrown off by a more dynamic strategy. That was what Lee outlined to his generals. While part of the Confederate army would be left as a decoy force to face McClellan's troops massed east of Richmond, Jackson would bring his men over from the Shenandoah Valley where they would join the rest of Lee's men north of Richmond and begin the drive to force McClellan to pull back.

There then ensued what would later become known as the Seven Days' Battles; to the Confederacy of the time, they were seven days that revived its hopes. Ironically, the first of these battles was begun by McClellan at Oak Grove, east of Richmond, when on 25 June, a day before Lee had planned to start his campaign, McClel-lan decided to move toward Richmond. A minor engagement as battles go, it turned out to fore-shadow the results of the remaining week. Another general might have decided to continue his drive the next day, so light was Confederate resistance. Lee, for his part, might have called off his own campaign, so potentially dangerous was this new Federal initiative. Instead, Lee simply proceeded on 26 June with his planned attack on a wing of the Federals up near Mechanicsville, a few miles north of Richmond. In some respects the battle was a near disaster for the Confederates, their casualties of some 1400 being four times that of the Federals, but Lee learned from it

Above: General James Longstreet, known as Lee's 'Old Work Horse,' fought at First Bull Run, in the Peninsular Campaign of 1862, at Fredericksburg, at Gettysburg, in the Wilderness Campaign in May 1864, and through to the end of the war.

Opposite: A portrait of Robert E Lee, whose masterly military campaign prevailed against the odds for a time.

Left: Major General George Brinton McClellan (1826-1885), whose conservative and defensive manner in the field Lee took great advantage of, commanded the Army of the Potomac until Lincoln replaced him in November 1862.

and refused to lose heart. The very next day, 27 June, Lee pursued the Federals to Gaines's Mill, about four miles southeast, down the Chickahominy River from Mechanicsville; again the Confederate forces took heavier casualties (some 8750 to the Federals' 6840), and again Lee's plans went awry in the heat of battle. He refused to panic, while McClellan pulled back still farther. The 28th saw no major engagement, primarily because Lee's forces could not find the Federals where they expected them to be making a stand. On the 29th units of Lee's army commanded by General John Magruder engaged the now retreating Federals, first at Allen's Farm, then at Savage's Station. When darkness and a thunderstorm ended the fighting, the Federals pulled out during the night, abandoning 2500 of their wounded in a field hospital, plus large amounts of supplies.

By this time it was clear that Lee's strategy was succeeding and that McClellan was heading for the James River. The Confederate forces caught up with the Federals at White Oak Swamp during the morning of the 30th. By the time the fighting broke off about nine o'clock that evening the Federals had hardly been overwhelmed, but they were hurt badly enough so that McClellan gave no thought to breaking off his retreat. The next day Lee's forces caught up with McClellan's at Malvern Hill, about halfway between White Oak Swamp and the point on the James River where the Federals were gathering. The Federals were well entrenched on the hill and had formidable artillery – it was late in the afternoon before Lee gave the command to mount a major attack. As too often before, staff and command confusion

John Bankhead Magruder (1810-1871), who mistakenly led his troops away from the battle at Malvern Hill, was blamed for contributing to the Confederate defeat. Magruder transferred to Texas in October.

cost the Confederates terribly. 'It was not war, it was murder,' said General D H Hill afterward. During that night McClellan withdrew his forces to Harrison's Landing on the James River. Richmond was saved: some 90,000 men of McClellan's Federal Army of the Potomac had been forced to abandon the Peninsular Campaign.

Lee was immediately hailed as the savior of the Confederacy, but he himself knew how close to failing his counteroffensive had come. The casualties alone had been staggering: of his force of 85,000 troops, some 19,000 were killed or wounded, another 1000 were missing. And as Lee himself wrote in his report on the campaign, 'Under ordinary circumstances, the Federal Army should have been destroyed.' Despite heavy losses the main force of the Federal army was free 'to recover and then recommence operations,' as Lee shrewdly observed. Lee had to take responsibility, and did, but he also learned that many of his generals simply could not be relied on for aggressive, independent, timely, decisive action. Lee learned many other things from the Seven Days' Battles. He had not used his artillery and cavalry to the best avail, he had failed to co-ordinate his various units in the field, he had failed to obtain 'correct and timely information.' Above all, he had learned that he could not remain so isolated during the actual battles: he had to be on the scene, giving active direction, inspiring and commanding his men.

Lee would have many occasions to test his

powers of command in the months that followed. Within two weeks of abandoning the pursuit of McClellan's army, in fact, Lee faced a new threat from the north, the advance of General John Pope's army from the northwest of Richmond. He dispatched Stonewall Jackson to head off this threat, thereby precipitating the Second Battle of Bull Run, or Manassas, as it is still known in the South. Although Jackson would be the chief commander in the various engagements, the campaign was essentially carried out under Lee's strategy. Particularly daring, not to say dangerous, was Lee's decision to divide his already far-outnumbered forces late in August with the intention of splitting the Federal line of communications. Had this plan failed to work, as it well might have, Lee could have lost his whole army. The campaign came to a climax on 29-30 August near the same creek at Manassas Junction where the Confederates had defeated the Federals in July 1861. Again thanks to Lee's willingness to commit his forces and to maneuver in the course of the battle, the Confederates won the day. In a further offensive, at Chantilly on 1 September, Lee forced Pope to withdraw his army all the way back to Washington.

Lee's next campaign, the invasion of Maryland, may have ended up costing Lee not only heavy casualties but the opposite of what he had hoped for. Besides the military goal of drawing Federal forces away from Virginia, Lee thought he might win over the border state of Maryland to the Confederate cause and even weaken the North's support of the war. Instead, after the climax Battle of Antietam (or Sharpsburg) on 17 September 1862 – 'the bloodiest single day of the war' as it would come to be known – Lee had to withdraw with a casualty count of some 20,000 dead, wounded, and missing. Perhaps more significant, Lincoln now issued the Emancipation Proclamation, which, by turning the war into a crusade to free the slaves, cost the Confederacy any potential support from Europe.

With winter approaching and his army in some disarray, Lee devoted the first weeks back in Virginia to reorganizing and resupplying his forces. In mid-November he learned that the Federal Army of the Potomac was on the move again, still aiming to take Richmond, this time by coming from the northwest. The Federals evidently intended to cross the Rappahannock River at Fredericksburg, a small city on its south bank, and although Lee would have preferred to make his stand elsewhere, he quickly moved his forces up to Fredericksburg. By early December Lee had some 78,000 men in position on the heights surrounding Fredericksburg, while across the river were the 122,000 Federals, now commanded by General Ambrose Burnside. Burnside's men began to put pontoon bridges across the river on 11 December; by the 13th he had over 100,000 men across and began an assault on the Confederate positions. It turned out to be a virtually suicidal effort, as wave after wave of the Federals were mowed down as the Confederates fired from the heights. It was on this occasion that

Above: The battle at Malvern Hill, north of Richmond, between Union forces under General McClellan and Confederate troops under Lee, Longstreet and Jackson, on 1 July 1862.

Overleaf: Major General Burnside's forces lay pontoon bridges across the Rappahannock at Fredericksburg in preparation for their ill-fated attack on the city.

Above: Union forces await the Confederates at a double line of breastworks thrown up on the night of 6 May, in the Wilderness near Chancellorsville.

Right: Commander of the Army of the Potomac, Joseph Hooker reorganized the army but was outmaneuvered by Lee at Chancellorsville, where his tactics lacked aggression and a concussion led to a temporary loss of command.

Lee, looking down on the slaughter from above, said, 'It is well that war is so terrible else men would learn to love it too much.' The Federals lost some 12,700 dead or wounded, the Confederates some 5300. Lee did not order a counter-attack when the Federals withdrew to their side of the river, because the Federal artillery was positioned on heights above the river. Furthermore, Lee did not know just how badly the Federals had been hurt, and they had an advantage of some 43,000 men.

Both armies then settled in for the winter. General Burnside was replaced as commander of the Army of the Potomac by General Joseph Hooker (a colorful figure who allegedly contributed the word 'hooker' to the English language because of the flock of female camp followers who trailed his army wherever it went). Hooker opened the 1863 campaign by first landing troops down near Fort Monroe, requiring Lee to send two of his divisions under General Longstreet to meet this threat. Meanwhile, Hooker had so many men that by late April he could set out with about a third of his 134,000-man army to attempt a so-called turning movement, that is, go up the Rappahannock River, cross at Kelly's Ford well above Fredericksburg, and then come down behind Lee, who was still defending the Fredericksburg-Richmond line. Lee had a total of only some 62,000 men when the Federals began their move on 28 April, but he took the daring chance and left 10,000 in position southeast of Fredericksburg, then moved the rest of his force about six miles west to head off Hooker's forces, who would be advancing through a region known as 'the Wilderness.' This was a large wooded area, thick with vines and underbrush and even more difficult to traverse because of the boggy streams.

One of its several small clearings was known as Chancellorsville, after the Chancellor family whose land this was, and General Hooker now took over the Chancellor house as his headquarters. These were the parameters of the confrontation that would be known as the Battle of Chancellorsville – Robert E Lee's greatest achievement as a general and universally esteemed as one of the world's military masterpieces.

Some of Lee's success is perhaps to be credited to Hooker's errors. For one, Hooker had sent his 10,000-man cavalry force under General George Stoneman on what turned out to be an all-but-useless ride around the Confederates' western flank. Hooker's plan was to draw off the Confederate cavalry under Jeb Stuart and so threaten Richmond that Lee would have to assign more troops to the capital's defense. In the end Stuart simply ignored the Federal cavalry, who ended up doing little more than destroying some railroad lines when they might have tipped the balance in the main battle at Chancellorsville. Hooker's other major error was a failure of nerve. After the first minor confrontation between his skirmishers and some Confederates on 1 May, Hooker ordered his vastly superior forces to pull back and take up a defensive position in the Wilderness. As Hooker himself would later admit, 'To tell the truth, I just lost faith in Joe Hooker.'

These failings, however, in no way detract from Lee's historic achievement. It began with his very willingness to go forth to meet such a superior force: he might well have chosen to remain entrenched at Fredericksburg and other positions around Richmond. Then came his bold gamble at splitting his already outnumbered force, leaving those 10,000 men under General Jubal Early to face a much larger force under General John Sedgwick while Lee directed the remaining 50,000 or so to go straight toward Hooker's advancing army. Lee's next daring move came on the morning of 2 May, when he sent General Jackson with some 30,000 men on a march around to the west to threaten the Federals' exposed flank; the remaining Confederates made feinting attacks to deceive the Federals massed along the eastern edge of the Wilderness.

Jackson moved some 25,000 men during the day with the Federals only some two-and-a-half miles to their right, but largely separated from the Confederates by heavy woods. Some Federal troops, finally aware of Jackson's movement, were unable to persuade Hooker that there was any real threat from this direction. He decided, in fact, that Jackson's men were retreating! Even when two Federal divisions fought a sharp little engagement with a rearguard regiment of Jackson's, Hooker did not change his appraisal of the situation.

By about four that afternoon Jackson had most of his force in position. He had already been taken to a vantage point where he could look down on the unsuspecting Federal troops relaxing in their camp. By six o'clock he gave the command to attack. Some 20,000 Confederates, giving the eerie Rebel yell and driving the forest animals before them, came charging out of the woods, and some 9000 Federals of the XI Corps, many of them German-Americans who barely spoke English, fled back towards Chancellorsville. One Federal division made something of a stand, but it too soon retreated. By eight o'clock Hooker had managed to bring other infantry and artillery into action and halt the Confederate advance. Lee, meanwhile, had continued to divert the enemy by making a number of attacks on the Federals east of Chancellorsville. Jackson, for his part, went reconnoitering in response to word that a large body of Hooker's forces were massing for a possible night attack. Refusing, with his usual impatience and determination to see things through himself, to heed the urging of his fellow officers to send someone else less indispensable to scout the territory, he got caught in a confusion of crossfire and was hit by a shell

A sketch by A R Waud of fighting in the Wilderness.

from his own men, who mistook him and his staff for Federal cavalry. Severely wounded, he had to be taken from the field and, after a harrowing journey in a wagon that passed for an ambulance, finally reached a doctor, who found it necessary to amputate his left arm below the shoulder.

About the same time that Jackson was undergoing surgery, one of his officers reported to Lee about the progress of the battle. Although the officer did not yet know how severely Jackson had been wounded, it was clear that he would not be able to carry out his command, nor would A P Hill, to whom Jackson had passed his command when taken from the field. For Hill himself received a wound which, if less serious than Jackson's proved to be, put him out of action. Lee immediately assigned Jeb Stuart to take over Jackson's troops, and by dawn on 3 May Stuart was leading an attack on Hooker's forces. By ten o'clock that morning Hooker's troops had to pull back from Chancellorsville. Lee and Stuart met at the Chancellor house as their two forces united, but barely had time to celebrate when word came that the holding force under Jubal Early's command on the heights above Fredericksburg had finally been dislodged by the greatly superior Federal force under John Sedgwick. Further, Sedgwick's Federals were at that very moment making their way westward toward Lee's rear. Lee immediately broke off his full-scale pursuit of Hooker and sent reinforcements back to Early's men. By that evening the Confederates had managed to halt Sedgwick's advance but the fact was that Lee's army was now essentially

caught between two Federal forces with about twice as many troops.

Lee had already defied the odds, not to mention most of the conventional rules of warfare, and most commanders would probably have withdrawn southward during the night, allowing the Federals to join up in the morning – and then possibly to launch another attack. But Lee was not made of the stuff of most commanders. He ordered yet another daring offensive. On the afternoon of 3 May he left Jeb Stuart with about 25,000 men to hold the forces under Hooker to the west (some 75,000 men) and then took 20,000 men to attack Sedgwick's force. Still displaying the ingenious tactics that had sustained the battle so long, Lee split his force and sent about half of them under General Richard Anderson around to the southern flank of Sedgwick. The next morning, as Early brought his regrouped force up to the eastern flank Lee moved in from the west. Sedgwick realized he was surrounded and retreated across a ford on the Rappahannock.

Lee still confronted Hooker's 75,000-man force well entrenched in the Wilderness to his west and might have been satisfied at least to pause and dig in. Instead, he planned to launch an attack on Hooker on 6 May. One of Lee's own generals put it most aptly: 'It must be conceded that Lee never in his life took a more audacious resolve than when he determined to assault Hooker's entrenchments. And it is the highest possible compliment to the army commanded by Lee to say that there were two persons who be-

A scene from the battle of Chancellorsville, Virginia, 3 May 1863.

lieved that, in spite of all the odds, it would have been victorious. These two persons were General Lee and General Hooker.' During the rainy night of 5 May Hooker withdrew his forces across the Rappahannock, and on 6 May Lee could look out upon a Virginia clear of Federal forces from the Wilderness to Richmond.

It had been a costly victory: the Confederates lost some 12,800 dead, wounded, or missing, the Federals 17,200. Percentagewise, however, the Federal casualties were only 13 percent of the force involved, whereas they were 22 percent of the Confederate force. Worst of all, however, was the loss of Stonewall Jackson – he died on 10 May from pneumonia. For Lee that loss was irreparable. 'I know not how to replace him,' he mourned. His greatest victory had been dimmed for him forever. No campaign he planned or carried out would ever again be the same without his closest, most trusted lieutenant.

As his men fell in for the march to Pennsylvania a short while after, Lee must often have asked himself: Can the Army continue to achieve success without Jackson?

Right: Battle artist Alfred R Waud.

Below: The wounded escaping from the burning woods of the Wilderness, May 1864.

Overleaf: Marye's Heights, Fredericksburg, Virginia, after the hill was taken by Sedgwick's 6th Maine Infantry on 3 April 1863.

Wounded escaping from the burning woods of the Wilderness –

GEORGE GORDON MEADE

Gettysburg

Pickett's Charge at
Gettysburg, 3 July 1863.

Above: Strategy is discussed at a Council of War held at the Executive Mansion.

In the year before Gettysburg the Union had fought four major battles under as many commanders: John Pope at Bull Run, George McClellan at Antietam, Ambrose Burnside at Fredericksburg, and Joseph Hooker at Chancellorsville. Clearly, things were not going well for the Army of the Potomac. President Lincoln, faced with Lee's unbroken string of victories, reluctantly contemplated yet another change of command after Hooker's defeat at Chancellorsville. Lincoln thought first of General John F Reynolds, but Reynolds flatly refused the command. Only then did Lincoln turn to George G Meade, an officer whose record was, if not undistinguished, by no means distinguished. Nonetheless, Meade had fought well at Fredericksburg, and had given signs that he would have fought well at Chancellorsville had Hooker given him the chance. Now, by appointing him commander of the Army of the Potomac, Lincoln was giving him that opportunity.

Clearly, Meade's appointment was a gamble, but after the senior, and perhaps more qualified Reynolds refused the command, Lincoln had little alternative. The steady attrition in Union commanders left Meade as the best choice, despite his unremarkable career. It is, in fact, hard to imagine a greater contrast than that between the two commanders at Gettysburg: Lee, who had gone from strength to strength, and Meade, the often short-tempered laborer in the vineyards, who had repeatedly seen promotion and glory elude him.

If Robert E Lee's family had had a whiff of scandal – his father's indebtedness, his half-brother's questionable personal life – Meade's family seemed to encapsulate the aphorism 'Rags to Riches to Rags' in three generations. Meade's grandfather, the son of Irish immigrants, was born in Philadelphia, which was to be the Meades' American home for generations. This first George Meade was a merchant, who made his fortune in the West Indies, and a patriot, who bankrolled the Pennsylvania Bank's effort to supply George Washington's hard-pressed army with food and clothing. Yet by 1801 George Meade was bankrupt, although his son, Richard Worsam Meade, was busily amassing a considerable fortune in Santo Domingo.

Richard Worsam Meade's success was such that in 1806 he was appointed United States naval agent to Cadiz, Spain, where his son George Gordon Meade was born on New Year's Eve 1815. Young George was not to know the pleasures of the privileged childhood enjoyed by his older brothers and sisters. In 1816 Richard Meade was imprisoned by the Spanish Government in the aftermath of the Peninsular War. The family's astonishing art collection, one of the first assembled by an American, and including works by Titian, Rubens, Van Dyke, and Velasquez, was sold. Soon all that would remain with George Gordon Meade from the good years was a lifelong love of classical music; years later, he would write poignantly of how he missed the solace of music while on campaign.

Her husband in prison, George's mother returned to Philadelphia with her children, and tried to minimize the effect on her young brood of their father's indebtedness and imprisonment. After his release from prison in 1818 Richard Meade returned to the United States and devoted all his time to trying to collect the $491,153.62 owed him by Spain. Understandably, this became an obsession with him, and he died disappointed and still bankrupt in 1828, leaving his wife with one overriding concern: how to educate young George.

A private university was obviously out of the question, and so Mrs Meade turned in despair to the military academy in the hope of securing a free education for her son. 'I offer my son, George Meade, as a candidate for the appointment of Cadet in the Military Academy,' she wrote to the Secretary of War in 1830. The application was initially refused, but when she tried again the next year, George, now sixteen, was accepted at West Point.

The fact that George Gordon Meade went to West Point to gain a free education, not to

Top: Generals George G Meade, John Sedgwick and Robert O Tyler with staff officers at the Horse Artillery Headquarters at Brandy Station, Virginia.

Above: President Lincoln and General Scott review a three-years regiment on Pennsylvania Avenue, as sketched by A R Waud.

prepare himself for a military career, is perhaps reflected in his record: at graduation Meade ranked 19 out of a class of 56 and had accumulated 168 demerits (200 would have meant expulsion). Although remembered by a classmate as being of the 'highest breeding,' this appraisal suggests a young man whose background, not his character or deeds, was still his strong suit.

With his undistinguished record, Meade saw little hope of advancement in a peacetime army and resigned his commission in 1836, only a year after graduation from West Point. Once more a civilian, Meade drew on his army training in surveying and engineering, working for the Topographical Bureau mapping the Texas-Louisiana border, and charting shoals in the Mississippi River Delta. Still, it was piecework, with intervals of unemployment, and, after his marriage in 1840, the pay was not sufficient to support a family. In 1842 Meade re-enlisted as a second lieutenant, uncomfortably aware that his classmates who had stayed in the army had already advanced to the rank of captain.

Soon Meade found himself in Texas, with Zachary Taylor's army, and then serving with General Winfield Scott in the Mexican War. Meade's topographical skills were put to good use, and he was brevetted a first lieutenant on 23 September 1846. The promotion was particularly sweet after previous disappointments, when citation in dispatches had led to promotion of others but not of Meade. In a letter to his wife, Meade had tried to make the best of his earlier disappointments. 'In truth, I have but little claim as far as the two battles are concerned,' he had written. 'I did my duty and my duty simply [and] . . . knowing how these things are done, I was fully prepared for my not being noticed.'

In the years following the Mexican campaign Meade continued his topographical work, constructing lighthouses in Delaware, Florida, and Michigan, worthy work, but hardly the best preparation for the battlefield. Indeed, when hostilities broke out and the Civil War began, there were those who whispered that Meade's promotion on 31 August 1861 to brigadier general in charge of one of the Pennsylvania brigades was due less to his military abilities than to his wife's political influence: Mrs Meade was the daughter of Congressman John Sergeant.

Even now, with the nation at war, Meade's contributions were initially as an engineer and surveyor, assisting in the construction of Fort Pennsylvania. However, in the Peninsular Campaign Meade finally saw action, and was twice wounded at White Oak Swamp, once in the arm and once, humiliatingly, in the back. Reassurances from the army doctor that the bullet had entered just as Meade twisted in his saddle mollified Meade. 'General Meade fought with great bravery and skill, and greatly added to his reputation as a soldier,' stated the *Philadelphia Press* when Meade returned home to recuperate from his wounds. Recuperate he did, returning to

active duty 50 days later, although the lingering effect of the bullet that entered through his back would weaken him and eventually contribute to his early death in 1872.

Meade was back in action for the Second Battle of Bull Run, and for South Mountain and Antietam. The man who had made his early career as a topographer was now beginning to make his mark as a tough fighter. Confederate General Daniel H Hill called Meade 'one of our most dreaded foes' after South Mountain, and at Antietam Meade took over command from Hooker when the latter collapsed during the battle. Now promotions began to come – to major general of volunteers and then to the command of

Above: Gilbert Gaul's painting, *Bringing up the Guns.*

Right: Samuel J Reader's depiction of the 300 2nd Kansas State Militia riding *Into the Jaws of Death.*

the Center Grand Division. By the time of Chancellorsville it was Meade, not the more battle-experienced General Joseph Hooker, who argued for an all-out assault on Confederate forces. As Union Colonel Alexander Webb later recalled, 'I have never known anyone so vehemently to advise an attack on the field of battle.' Hooker ignored Meade's exhortations but, after the battle, when Lincoln heard that Meade had pressed the attack, he remembered, and determined to offer Meade the supreme command. As President Lincoln said (with his customary earthiness) to Secretary of War Stanton, if the fighting were to be in Pennsylvania, Meade would fight well 'on his own dunghill.'

It was clear that Lee had won a great, if costly, victory at Chancellorsville. However, much was unclear in the days after that great battle. Neither Lee and the Army of Northern Virginia nor the battered Joe Hooker and the Army of the Potomac were sure where the other's main forces were deployed. What would be the first move, and who would make it? This was the question that Jefferson Davis and Abraham Lincoln, Robert E Lee and Joseph Hooker were asking themselves and their advisers. Ironically, the man who would command the Union forces in the war's next great engagement, Gettysburg, General George Meade, was not then privy to the highest councils of war.

If matters in the northern war theater were critical, the situation in the west was no less so. Since late April Grant had been pressing toward Vicksburg, Mississippi, in the hope both of seizing the critical port itself and of dividing the Confederacy. If Union forces could control strategic Mississippi ports such as Vicksburg and Port Hudson, the Confederacy would be severely weakened.

On 30 May the two most important leaders of the besieged Confederacy, Lee and Jefferson Davis, met at Richmond to discuss the situation. Both feared that Vicksburg (and, with it, much of the South's western flank) might soon be lost. Both feared the intentions of General Hooker and his enormous force. For Lee, at least, if a choice had to be made between saving Vicksburg and the west or Virginia, there was no choice at all. For Lee, his home state of Virginia *was* the Confederacy.

The moment called for boldness and daring, for speed and tactical genius. Lee determined on an invasion of the north. 'I considered the problem in every possible phase,' he later wrote,

Opposite: President Lincoln and his staff.

Above: General Sigel's Corps at the Second Battle of Bull Run, fought 29 August 1862.

Left: A depiction of General John Reynolds by Max Rosenthal. Reynolds refused the commission which Meade accepted.

Once the decision was made, a midnight messenger was sent from Lincoln in Washington to Meade in Frederick, Maryland, arriving on 28 June, at three in the morning. When Meade was awakened and told that someone from the War Office was there to see him, he thought for one dreadful moment that he was under arrest for opposing Hooker at Chancellorsville. It took some hours for the news to sink in. 'Why not Reynolds?' Meade asked, only to learn that Reynolds had refused the command, fearing that he would not be given a free hand. Meade composed himself, and accepted the command he had never expected, and seemed now not to want. Within days he would be leading the Army of the Potomac in the greatest battle of the war, a little-known commander at a little-known town: Gettysburg.

Above: Union forces advancing at Antietam, September 1862.

Right: General Joseph Hooker, whom Meade replaced as Commander of the Army of the Potomac.

'and to my mind, it resolved itself into a choice of one of two things: either to retire to Richmond and stand a siege, which must ultimately have ended in surrender, or to invade Pennsylvania.'

An invasion of enemy territory had much to recommend it: Lee would move his troops, sorely in need of provisions, into Pennsylvania, where they could live off the land, not of exhausted Southern farmers, but of unscathed Northerners. Lee analyzed his decision in these terms: 'An invasion of the enemy's country breaks up all his preconceived plans, relieves our country of his presence, and we subsist there while on his resources. The question of food for this army gives me more trouble and uneasiness than everything else combined; the absence of the army from Virginia gives our people an opportunity to collect supplies ahead.' However, unlike Sherman and Sheridan later in the war, Lee gave strict orders to his men to pay for all goods they received from farmers and under no circumstances to do harm to farmers or their families. And he saw that his orders were obeyed – in one instance he had two of his soldiers hanged for robbing and killing a farmer.

At the same time, Lee hoped, the presence of the Army of Northern Virginia north of the Potomac might so thoroughly strike terror into the Union that there would be a groundswell of sentiment for ending the war. Then too, perhaps a great victory would finally gain that elusive goal of the Confederacy: international recognition. In short, Lee hoped again that he could drive 'our enemies back to their homes' and change 'the character of the war.'

On 3 June Lee and the Army of Northern Virginia moved north from Fredericksburg. The Federal Army of the Potomac under General Joseph Hooker waited and watched. And that tactic, as much as anything, led to President Lincoln's decision on 27 June to remove General Hooker from command of the Army of the Potomac and to appoint General George Meade in his place. By then Lee's men, beginning on 17 June, had crossed over the Potomac; as Confederate soldiers would recall later, they had 'breakfast in Virginia, whiskey in Maryland, and supper in Pennsylvania.' The situation confronting General George Meade on 28 June was that of the enemy settling in indefinitely to have breakfast, whiskey, and supper in Pennsylvania, unless he could stop them.

Immediately, Meade determined to move north. Uncertain as to whether Lee would stand and fight in Pennsylvania or sweep down on Maryland and Washington, Meade halted the main force of his army for the night of 28 June at Pipe Creek. From Pipe Creek Meade knew that he could quickly cross into Pennsylvania, or wheel and protect Washington and Maryland. All day there had been skirmishes around Chambersburg, Pennsylvania, and Lee decided to forego an assault on Harrisburg. Instead, he made for Gettysburg, a market town whose only signifi-

A trooper, with typical equipment and uniform, of 6th New York Cavalry Regiment.

A scene from the Battle of Gettysburg, 3 July 1863.

cance was that it was traversed by major north-south and east-west roads.

Intelligence on both sides was scanty. Lee's 'eyes', Jeb Stuart, had set off with his cavalry on 25 June to ride round the Federal troops, gather information, and join up with Lee in two days. 'Can you tell me where General Stuart is?' Lee asked repeatedly on the 28th and the days that followed. It was not until one o'clock in the morning on 2 July that Stuart regained Lee's main force – and, by then, it was too late.

For Meade the intelligence he was getting was equally inadequate and particularly frustrating for a man trained in topography and who, during the Mexican campaign, used to saddle up and ride behind enemy lines to do his own scouting. Yet for once Meade's hot temper was in check. 'I have seen him,' wrote a colleague, 'so cross and ugly that no one dared to speak to him – in fact, at such times his staff and everybody else kept as clear of him as possible.' Fortunately, in the Gettysburg campaign, the general who confessed to hearing his own soldiers once call him a 'd———d old goggle-eyed snapping turtle' was calm, cool, and determined, and perhaps not a little aware of the gentlemanly reputation of his opponent, Robert E Lee, who had stated that he intended to 'carry on the war in Pennsylvania without violating the sanctions of a high civilization and of Christianity.'

On the 29th, concerned that his forces were stretched too thin, Lee sent word to his far-flung units to head for Gettysburg. Meade, by now convinced that Lee would not head south, himself headed north. To his wife he wrote, 'We are marching as fast as we can to relieve Harrisburg but have to keep a sharp lookout that the rebels don't turn around and get at Washington and Baltimore in our rear.... I am going straight at them, and will settle this thing one way or another.'

It was an unseasonably hot day. Sunstroke laid many soldiers low; most marched in their underwear, carrying their heavy uniforms. The next day was even hotter, but by nightfall Meade's closest friend, General John Reynolds, had moved into and secured the town of Gettysburg. Meade himself was 14 miles away at Taneytown. That night Union and Confederate forces had

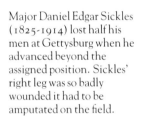

Major Daniel Edgar Sickles (1825-1914) lost half his men at Gettysburg when he advanced beyond the assigned position. Sickles' right leg was so badly wounded it had to be amputated on the field.

the last good night's sleep they would have until after the three-day battle, a battle that would leave more than 7000 young soldiers fallen on the field.

Incredibly, it was not until the morning of 1 July that Meade finally received a topographical map of Pennsylvania. Irritatingly, he had mislaid the spectacles that had earned him the nickname of 'old goggle eyes' and had to squint to make out the map's unfamiliar terrain. While Meade was studying the map, in an attempt to predict Lee's strategy, a messenger arrived from General Reynolds with the news that 'The enemy are advancing in strong force.' The battle, it seemed, had begun.

Meade had hardly had time to digest Reynolds's frantic message when a second, more somber, message arrived: Reynolds himself was dead, one of Gettysburg's first casualties, picked off by a sharpshooter who had recognized the general's flamboyant white shirt. Meade was stunned, but sent off General Winfield S Hancock to replace the fallen Reynolds. En route to Gettysburg, Hancock was passed by the horse-drawn ambulance bringing Reynolds's body back behind the lines. It was hardly a good omen for General George Meade and the Army of the Potomac.

It was not until almost 10:00 that evening that Meade headed off for Gettysburg, arriving, under a rising moon, about midnight. General Oliver O Howard briefed his commander on how the day's fighting had gone: it had not gone well.

All day the Confederate forces had had the advantage of initiative and attack, while the Union troops had been forced to react and defend positions they were boxed into. Lee's scattered forces, now galvanized, attacked from all directions, making it impossible for the numerically superior Union army to unite. Union General Howard had been forced back first in heavy fighting along Cemetery Ridge and at Cemetery Hill, and, finally, in the fields around the Lutheran Seminary.

Ultimately, Union forces were driven south of Gettysburg itself, and the town was now in Confederate hands. Union casualties had been heavy, especially among Major General John Buford's cavalry, which had seen the first action of the day, and among General Abner Doubleday's Iron Brigade, which suffered casualties of 80 percent. More than 4000 Union soldiers had been taken prisoner, although in the one Federal triumph of the day, at the railroad bridge by the Chambersburg Road, 400 Confederate soldiers were taken prisoner.

In fact, it could be, and was, argued later that had the Confederate command, especially General R S Ewell and Lee himself, pressed home the attack at day's end, the Battle of Gettysburg might have been a one- not a three-day battle, with a Confederate, not a Union victory. As it was, the one thing that was certain was that 2 July would bring renewed fighting; from Cemetery

Ridge Meade surveyed the potential battlefield, and ordered reinforcements to the heights at Little and Big Round Top and Culp's Hill. Finally, Meade retired to his command headquarters at Widow Leister's two-room white frame farmhouse near the Union front line.

The initiative was still with Lee on the second day of the battle of Gettysburg. While General James Longstreet urged that Lee sweep round Meade's forces and attack from the rear, Lee, uncharacteristically, chose a more conservative plan: he would attack Meade's flanks in the hope of collapsing the Union line. Had Stuart been with him, had Lee known Meade's exact position – above all, had the indomintable Jackson survived to do battle with him – Lee might have been able to follow Longstreet's bold suggestion.

As it was, fighting did not begin until midafternoon, by which time the fierce summer sun was parching the already exhausted Union and Confederate soldiers. Major Daniel E Sickles had, against orders, moved the Union III Corps out from Little Round Top and Cemetery Ridge into a peach orchard and wheatfield below, where he and his men were almost immediately attacked by Longstreet's full force of 12,000 to 14,000 men, supported by artillery. 'The slaughter beat all I had ever seen,' a soldier later recalled.

Sickles's men retreated to an indeterminate rocky outcropping soon named 'Devil's Den,' where many attempted to take shelter in crevices and fissures. Long after the battle dead Union soldiers were found within the folds of Devil's Den, dead without a wound on them, killed by the force of the concussion of Longstreet's heavy artillery. It was just as well that Father William Corby, chaplain of the Irish Brigade, had given the entire brigade general absolution when he realized the dire straits his men were in.

Meade sent reinforcements to aid Sickles's decimated troops in a desperate attempt to reclaim the abandoned Little Round Top. So many horses had been killed that foot soldiers had to drag artillery up Little Round Top, through terrain difficult to climb unburdened. In the fighting fully 80 per cent of the First Minnesota Brigade fell, but Little Round Top was regained, a strategic eminence that Sickles should never have abandoned.

The fighting was no less fierce at Culp's Hill, where Union forces stood firm while Confederate soldiers stormed up the hill, through the dense woods, again and again, with fearful casualties. One who fell was Wesley Culp, a native of Gettysburg and a relative of the man who owned the land Culp's Hill stood on. Work had taken Culp to Virginia, and, when the war broke out, he had enlisted in the 2nd Virginia Regiment. Now, once more at Gettysburg, Wesley Culp had visited his mother and sisters before the battle broke out, then rejoined his regiment. On 2 July, in the Confederate assault on Culp's hill, a favorite family picnic spot in his youth, Wesley Culp was shot dead. Young Culp's story is as good a symbol as any of the way the Civil War arbitrarily pitted neighbor against neighbor, brother against brother. Indeed, several of General Meade's sisters and daughters had married Southerners, and the army he led at Gettysburg was bent on winning a victory that would sadden members of his own family.

Fighting stopped in the early evening of 2 July, and as stillness fell over the battlefield, the horrible cries of the wounded for help and for water replaced the din of battle. Once more Meade met with his senior staff at his headquarters at Widow Leister's farmhouse. The day had almost been lost by Sickles's insubordinate

The Peach Orchard, painted by F D Briscoe, depicts the bloody fighting at the Angle in Gettysburg, Pennsylvania.

Left, below and *right:* Three days of fierce fighting at Gettysburg ended on 3 July 1863. In the costliest battle of the war, the Confederates lost 3903 killed, 18,735 wounded and 5425 missing, for a total of 28,063 – a third of Lee's army – while the Federals lost 3155 killed, 14,529 wounded and 5365 missing, for a total of 23,049.

Opening engagement.

Relieving with prolonge.

Shelled out.

Position on the 3rd and 4th July.

Leaving the field. July 5th.

Above: F D Briscoe's painting, *Charge of the Louisiana Tigers*, depicts a dramatic scene from the Battle of Gettysburg.

Below: Major General George Edward Pickett led the fateful charge against Union lines on the third day of battle at Gettysburg, as ordered by Lee.

and ill-advised actions, but by nightfall Meade could say in relief 'It is all right now!' The staff agreed to stand firm and fight on the morrow, although after the battle some, friends perhaps of Sickles, alleged that Meade had been ready to retreat and concede the victory to Lee.

It does not seem likely, for Meade, as his colleague Colonel W R Livermore later stated, 'was not original in devising brilliant plans, but his clear understanding enabled him to discriminate between the plans of others.' At no time was this ability of Meade's more evident than on the night of 2 July, when he realized that Lee must now attack the Union center. Aides were less sure: Was not the Union center its strongest

point? It was, Meade acknowledged, but, as he stated, Lee 'has made attacks on both our flanks and failed, and if he concludes to attack again it will be on our center.' It only remained to wait for dawn and learn whether Lee would, in fact, attack. His losses had already been enormous in men and material, but the tide of battle was thus far favorable for the Army of the Confederacy. Morning would reveal Lee's decision and Meade's reaction.

Lee's plan was simple: Jeb Stuart, finally on the spot, should harass Meade's rear while Ewell continued the assault on Culp's Hill, and, most critically, Longstreet should attack the center of the Union forces. In fact, Ewell jumped the gun,

much as Sickles had the day before, and the three-pronged attack opened with an abortive skirmish on Culp's Hill. Then all was quiet, a quiet remembered by all who were there as an unearthly quiet, deep and profound, and quiet particularly in contrast to what followed, the concerted firing of the Confederate artillery. Later, no one could say for sure how long the 140-gun cannonade had lasted: an hour? three hours? All that could be said was that nothing like it had been heard, or seen, before in North America. In fact, while the bombardment lasted, nothing could be seen but the swirling smoke and dust. All that saved Meade was the fact that the Confederate gunners could not see that their best shots were going too far, just over Union lines. In fact, Meade had to move his headquarters from the Widow Leister's farmhouse after it took several shells.

Finally, the artillery stopped, and through the smoke and dust, straight at the heart of Meade's army, just as he had predicted, came Lee's men, commanded by Longstreet, led by General George Pickett. It was Pickett's Charge – 15,000 soldiers heading straight for the heart of the Union army, bent on winning not only the battle but the war.

Now Meade let loose with the Union artillery, and the 15,000 men, marching in perfect formation, marched on, into the Valley of the Shadow of Death. They were raked by flanking fire, yet still marched on. When all seemed about to be lost, the dashing General Lewis A Armistead, his hat held above his head on his saber so that his men could see him, pressed forward and broke the Union lines. This was the moment forever to be remembered as the 'high water mark' of the Confederacy. Within minutes Armistead was fatally shot, the Confederate attack was broken, and men began to fall back in retreat.

The confusion was utter. Some Confederate units, blinded by the smoke, mistakenly fired on their comrades. Others fought fiercely to join comrades, only to discover themselves joining up with Union, not Confederate, units.

By late afternoon, when Meade rode out on the field, he was told that the Confederate attack had been stopped. Again, as when he had learned of his command only days earlier. Meade could not believe the news: 'What! Is the assault already repulsed?' It was. As Meade dashed off a note to his wife ('Papa is all safe, a splendid victory'), Lee walked down to meet his returning men, repeating over and over, 'It was all my fault.'

The greatest battle of the war, to date, or thereafter, had ended. Meade had taken an unsuccessful army from a string of unsuccessful commanders and won a great victory. Meade had once said, 'I like fighting as little as any man.' Yet at Gettysburg Meade had defeated the soldier's soldier. He would be criticized by many, including, initially, President Lincoln, for not exploiting the defeat and pursuing Lee's retreating army, but Meade was untroubled: 'The longer this war

continues,' he wrote, 'the more will Gettysburg be appreciated.'

After Gettysburg Meade continued in command of the Army of the Potomac, in a personally difficult tandem with the more illustrious Ulysses S Grant. Grant was aware that this was not easy for Meade, and later stated that Meade was 'so finely formed that if ordered to resign [his] general's commission and take service as [a] corporal, [he] would have fallen into the ranks without a murmur.' Indeed, when Philip Sheridan was appointed a lieutenant general of the army, Meade knew again the same disappointment of being passed over for promotion that had dogged his early military career.

Still, the Union had been saved because of Gettysburg, and Meade was the man who had done it. Never loved by his men as Lee was, never admired as was Grant, Meade had nonetheless redeemed his family's honor and had prevented the dismemberment of the country his grandfather had helped create.

At the war's end Meade stayed on in the army until 1869, serving during reconstruction, but he got most pleasure from his duties as commissioner of Fairmont Park, in his ancestral home of Philadelphia. It was on a walk there with his wife that Meade's old back wound acted up, signaling the onset of the pneumonia that brought his death on 6 November 1872. George Gordon Meade was, in his own words, 'a *juste-milieu* man,' and one who, although he liked fighting 'as little as any man,' had fought as well as any man when his country's fate hung in the balance at Gettysburg.

Above: Pickett's charge. Three Confederate prisoners at Gettysburg.

Ulysses S Grant

Shiloh
Vicksburg

The siege of Vicksburg – the fight in the crater of Fort Hill after the explosion, 25 June 1863.

Above: The batteries at Fort Donelson, on the Cumberland River, inflicted heavy damage on Union gunboats.

Below: Ulysses S Grant and his wife, the former Julia Dent, with their children.

On 7 November 1861 Ulysses S Grant, appointed brigadier general of volunteers by President Abraham Lincoln only three months before, attacked the Confederates at Belmont, Missouri, with 3100 green troops in an assault that was ill planned and poorly executed: it nearly ruined a promising career. Typically, Grant had not been ordered to attack, but only to make a 'demonstration,' an ostentatious movement that was supposed to appear menacing without leading to any real fighting.

Like most Northerners at this stage in the war, the aggressive-minded Grant believed that 'The rebellion would collapse suddenly and soon if a decisive victory could be gained over any of its armies.' Unlike most Northern generals, however, he was eager to get on with it. After a brief period of disfavor following Belmont, he was to have his chance. Taking note that the Confederate line stretching from Bowling Green, Kentucky, to Columbus was lightly guarded at its center by Fort Henry on the Tennessee River and Fort Donelson on the Cumberland, Grant proposed to cut the enemy's forces in two by capturing these forts. Their seizure would open routes of invasion along the Tennessee and Cumberland as the first step of the Union offensive in Tennessee.

Grant's second proposal, on 28 January 1862, to proceed against these forts, in which he was joined by Commodore Andrew Hull Foote, was approved by commanding General Henry W Halleck, who hoped the capture of the forts would force the abandonment of Columbus, a stronghold considered too formidable to attack. Grant and Foote, who had had armored vessels built especially for such actions, moved out promptly. On 6 February Foote's gunboats took the sparsely manned Fort Henry before Grant's force of about 17,000 could traverse the muddy terrain to join the attack. Although thus far Grant had been authorized to take only Fort Henry, and his request to Halleck to proceed to Fort Donelson was neither approved nor disapproved by the cautious commander, he marched as soon as possible to Fort Donelson, 12 miles away, where he was soon rejoined by Foote's fleet.

On 12 February Grant invested Fort Donelson, then manned by about 17,000 Confederate soldiers. Foote attacked from the river on 14 February, but was severely wounded and forced to retire. The next day, while Grant was conferring with Foote aboard his flagship, the Confederates, completely surrounded on land, staged an attack and by noon had opened up an escape route toward Clarksville. Grant returned to find his men ready to bolt, a staff officer white with fear, his right and center in utter confusion. Displaying the simple, direct style for which he was to become known, Grant galloped among his troops

shouting, 'Fill your cartridge boxes quick, and get into line; the enemy is trying to escape, and he must not be permitted to do so.' Grant's presence and self-control rallied the Federal soldiers, and his assault was a success. By nightfall the Union troops had possession of the outer Confederate trenches, and Donelson was hopelessly besieged.

Simon Bolivar Buckner, one of Grant's close friends before the war, had asked for terms of surrender. Grant replied, 'No terms except an immediate and unconditional surrender can be accepted. I propose to move immediately upon your works.' With these words, he leapt from utter obscurity to national prominence, earning the nickname 'Unconditional Surrender Grant.' The capture of Forts Henry and Donelson, with over 14,000 prisoners taken, was the North's first major victory. Grant, who had been appointed brigadier general of volunteers at his congressman's request, was named major general of volunteers by Abraham Lincoln, who began to follow this aggressive general closely.

Ulysses S Grant, born Hiram Ulysses Grant in 1822 in Ohio, was the son of Jesse Root Grant, a tanner descended from Grants who had arrived in Massachusetts in 1630, and Hannah Simpson, also of old and undistinguished American stock, a withdrawn, quiet, apparently emotionless woman whom young Ulysses resembled in stolidity. From infancy he hated the sight and smells of the bloody skins his father used in his trade. He never hunted, saying he could not bear to kill things, and further distinguished himself by refusing to use the rough language common to frontier boys.

Jesse Grant, a self-made man who had received only the most rudimentary education, was determined that his sons should be educated. Ulysses, however, showed no scholarly bent and was generally considered a dullard except for his skill in handling horses. When his father bought farmland outside Georgetown, Ohio, Ulysses, unwilling to work in the thriving tannery, spent most of his days with the horses, clearing land and hauling wood. It may have been here in the wilderness, with no one to ask questions or help make decisions, that Ulysses developed the

Above: The Federal gunboat attack on the water batteries of Fort Donelson. The armored vessels involved were the USS *Tyler, Conestoga, Carondolet, Pittsburg, Louisville* and *St Louis.*

Left: Confederate General Simon Bolivar Buckner, one of Grant's close friends before the war, commanded 17,000 men at Fort Donelson, many of them members of the garrison which had escaped from Fort Henry.

commonsense approach to life and the self-reliance that later characterized him.

When Ulysses was seventeen, his father secured him an appointment at West Point as a replacement for a cadet from the district who had flunked out. Everyone in Georgetown expected Ulysses to do likewise. Grant himself had no interest in a military career. His only purpose at the academy, he once remarked, was 'to get through the course, secure a detail for a few years as assistant professor of mathematics at the academy, and afterwards obtain a permanent position as a professor at some respectable college.' Unable to learn to march properly (he never danced), he finished 21st in a class of 39, and although he made some friends, he made no impression on anyone except for his superb riding and his ability to handle any horse in any situation. His Congressman had registered him as Ulysses Simpson Grant, an irretrievable change of name he accepted without much fuss, for it saved him from the possibility of being teased for the initials of his given H U G. After upperclassman William Tecumseh Sherman, viewing the

Above: The Battle of Shiloh (or Pittsburg Landing), Tennessee.

Below: Grant's success at Forts Henry and Donelson attracted favorable attention from President Lincoln.

list of new cadets, decided that 'U S Grant' stood for 'Uncle Sam Grant,' West Point and everyone who knew him at West Point called him 'Sam Grant.'

Following graduation as a brevet 2nd lieutenant, Grant was assigned to the infantry and stationed near St Louis, Missouri, where he met and fell in love with Julia Dent, sister of a West Point classmate. He served with exceptional bravery in the Mexican War, a conflict he felt entirely unjust, and saw action under General Zachary Taylor, whose informal dress and lack of military pretension may have served as a model for Grant's own generalship. After Taylor, Grant fought under General Winfield Scott, and was brevetted 1st lieutenant and then captain for bravery at Chapultepec. Grant learned practical warfare in Mexico and became acquainted with some of the men who were to command Confederate armies. Colonel Robert E Lee, an officer on Scott's staff, once reprimanded Grant for slovenly dress. (Later, as adversaries, these two would develop great respect for one another.)

After marrying his Julia and spending four happy years in New York and in Michigan, Grant had to leave his beloved wife and family behind when his regiment was transferred to the West Coast. Here he suffered from separation, boredom, and the knowledge that his pay was inadequate to support his family or to bring them to him. He failed at several attempts to increase his income, and began drinking. Faced with the prospect of a court-martial for repeated drunkenness, he resigned from the army in 1854. Secretary of War Jefferson Davis accepted his resignation without comment. Grant then failed at business in San Francisco. Charity got him to New York, where Academy classmate and Mexican-campaign comrade Simon Bolivar Buckner, whom he next met at Fort Donelson, guaranteed his hotel bill and lent him the money to rejoin his family.

Back in Missouri, Grant failed to make a go of the 80-acre farm his father-in-law gave him and bottomed out in real estate in St Louis. With a family to feed and nowhere else to go, he swallowed his pride and took a position in his brothers' leather goods store in Galena, Illinois,

where he bumbled so many sales that he was relegated to clerical work at a desk out of sight of customers. When war broke out, he organized Galena's first company of Union volunteers. The US Government refused him command of a regiment in May 1861, but Grant embarked on the action he longed for when Governor Richard Yates appointed him commander of the 21st Illinois Regiment. He cut such a shoddy figure when he took command that his troops ridiculed him to his face.

Grant's theory of war was simple: 'Find out where your enemy is. Get at him as soon as you can. Strike at him as hard as you can and as often as you can, and keep moving on.' For him the art of war consisted of the destruction of the enemy's principal army, an objective he understood better than any Northern general.

Assuming command of the Union Army of the Mississippi on 17 March 1862, Grant found his 38,000 troops in two encampments on the Tennessee River, part at the small town of Savannah, Tennessee, and part nine miles above on the west bank of the river near Pittsburg Landing. With the exception of General Lew Wallace's division of 5000 men, which was left at Crump's Landing, five miles below, Grant ordered the concentration of all his troops at Pittsburg Landing. There they were to be joined by General Don Carlos Buell's 25,000-man Army of the Ohio, which was marching southwest from Nashville. Grant's plan was to move with both armies against the northern Mississippi town of Corinth, where the vital Confederate railway line that led east from Memphis, connecting the western part of the Confederacy with Virginia, crossed the north-south line of the Mobile and Ohio.

Above: High-ranking Union officers, including Generals Winfield Scott (center, on white horse) and U S Grant (on rearing horse in foreground).

Left: A portrait of Grant made after his triumph at Vicksburg, Mississippi, which severed the Confederacy on the North-South axis and guaranteed its ultimate defeat (July 1863).

Grant and his most trusted subordinate, William Tecumseh Sherman, were aware that a numerically superior Confederate Army of the Mississippi under the highly regarded General Albert Sidney Johnston had been assembled at Corinth, only 25 miles away from Pittsburg Landing, but neither knew that Johnston, acting on accurate intelligence, planned to destroy Grant's army before Buell could reach him. Grant had not the slightest fear that Johnston's 40,000 'would leave strong entrenchments to take the initiative,' and he and his division commanders felt that it would be bad for morale to have their troops entrench. On 5 April Grant remarked, 'There willl be no fighting at Pittsburg Landing; we will have to go to Corinth.' That evening he

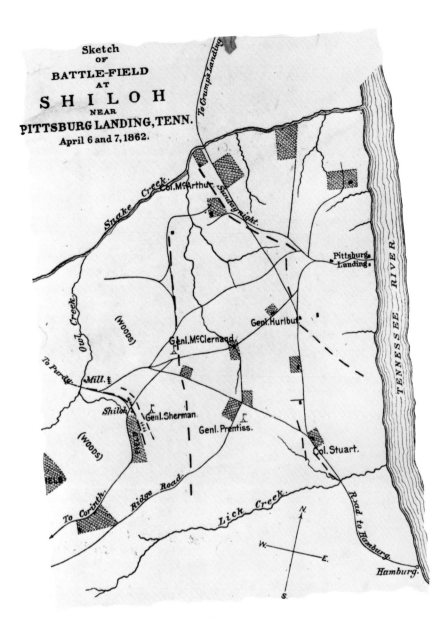

Sketch
OF
BATTLE-FIELD
AT
SHILOH
NEAR
PITTSBURG LANDING, TENN.
April 6 and 7, 1862.

Above: A sketch of the battleground at Shiloh, intersected by Owl, Snake and Lick Creeks and heavily wooded over much of its area.

Right: Recapture of artillery at Shiloh by men of General Rosseau's command, as depicted by Alonzo Chappel.

wired Halleck, 'I have scarcely the faintest idea of an attack being made upon us, but will be prepared should such a thing take place.'

Meanwhile Johnston's army had moved to within two miles of the Union lines. After sleeping on their guns, the Confederates attacked at five in the morning on 6 April; Johnston hoped to envelop the Union left flank by the river, cutting off reinforcements from Buell, and then to push the Federals back to Owl Creek, forcing a surrender. Grant, on crutches and lame from a riding accident, had left camp before dawn to have breakfast and meet with Buell in Savannah. When he heard the battle begin, he hurried onto a gunboat, and arrived at Pittsburg Landing about 8:30 AM to find thousands of terrified Federal soldiers huddled under the river bluffs, where they had been driven by the Rebels from their coffee pots. A total Confederate victory seemed imminent.

Grant sent an urgent appeal to Buell, whom he had not had time to meet; ordered his vanguard division under General William 'Bull' Nelson to move to the east bank of the Tennessee opposite Pittsburg Landing; and ordered Wallace to bring his division up from Crump's Landing. The cavalry was left to stop stragglers at gunpoint, if necessary, reorganize them, and return them to the fight.

Above: A Sunday morning service in the camp of the 69th New York. Such religious observances helped sustain the combatants on both sides and were commemorated in 'The Battle Hymn of the Republic': 'I can read His righteous sentence [the Scriptures] by the dim and flaring lamps, His day is marching on.'

Right: General Grant rallies forces at Shiloh, the first epic land battle of the Civil War. Casualties for both sides approached 24,000.

As he rode from division to division gathering firsthand information and encouraging commanders and troops, Grant realized that his adversary's attack had degenerated into a disorderly push all along the Union front, and that the Union forces had steadied and were withdrawing in rather good order. Fierce resistance from the Union center mounted by Benjamin Prentiss, whose men poured a killing fire from a sunken road the Rebels dubbed the 'Hornet's Nest,' was causing Johnston's original attack plan to lose momentum. With his left and right wings falling back, Grant realized his only hope was the delaying action of his center. He ordered Prentiss to hold 'at all hazards.'

After six hours of savage fighting and twelve Rebel assaults, during one of which Confederate commander Johnston receive a ball in his leg that cut an artery and cost him his life, Prentiss surrendered at 5:30 PM with the remaining half of his division – 2200 men. But even his surrender delayed and confused the Confederates, and Grant, although pushed back to the river, had time to form a defensive line studded with artillery at Pittsburg Landing. As the Confederates approached, Union gunboats *Lexington* and *Tyler* backed him up with heavy cannon fire. But the final assault never came. The Confederates, now under the command of General P G T Beauregard, awaiting the imminent arrival of General Earl Van Dorn with 20,000 reinforcements from Arkansas, had also received erroneous intelligence that Buell could not be expected to arrive in time to aid Grant. Beauregard decided to finish Grant off the next day.

Under cover of darkness Lew Wallace's division arrived from Crump's Landing, and Buell's 25,000 fresh troops crossed the river to join Grant. Night fell with a driving rain. Grant was offered refuge in a field hospital set up in a log house, but as he could never stand the sight of blood and amputations or the cries of the dying, he preferred to spend the night sitting under a tree in the rain. Alone there, he made plans for a well–co-ordinated attack the next morning.

At 7:30 AM on 1 April 1862 Grant threw his entire army forward against Beauregard. By 10:30 the Federals had regained most of the ground they had lost the day before. The focal point of the battle became the crossroads at Shiloh meeting house, now Beauregard's headquarters, along which Van Dorn's reinforcements could be expected to arrive, and which also might serve as a route of retreat to Corinth, if it came to that. As the relentless Federal attack pushed the Confederates farther back, Beauregard learned that Van Dorn's 20,000 men had been halted by the swollen Mississippi and would not arrive. He ordered a retreat for 3:00 PM. At about the same time, Grant, forbidding his men to open fire until they were well within musket range, personally organized the last Federal charge. The Confederates withdrew toward Corinth in the face of this onslaught; the Federals were too exhausted to give pursuit that day. General 'Old Brains' Halleck took command from Grant after the battle, and after amassing 100,000 troops, managed to consume four weeks covering the 20 miles to Corinth, stopping each night, to construct elaborate fortifications. By the time he reached Corinth, Beauregard, of course, was gone.

Shiloh was the largest and bloodiest battle on the American continent to that date, the first known battle in the Western Hemisphere to

Above: The Hornet's Nest was the center of Union resistance at Shiloh. Confederate forces attacked the position over a dozen times before its defenders surrendered.

Opposite top: Union forces were almost overwhelmed under the bluffs of the Tennessee River, near Pittsburg Landing (6-7 April 1862).

Far right: The Union flag comes under fire.

Near right: Union General William S Rosecrans, who fought with Grant at Corinth and was subsequently appointed to command of the Army of the Cumberland.

Below: Henry W Halleck, a cautious commander whom Lincoln appointed 'general-in-chief' in 1862, then demoted to chief-of-staff to make room for the more aggressive Grant (March 1864). In fact, Halleck was better suited to administration than to field command.

involve over 100,000 men. It was characterized by inept generalship on both sides, and great courage on the part of the enlisted men, over 80 percent of whom were green and untrained. The casualties in this 'soldiers' battle' were appalling: 13,047 for the North, 10,6794 for the South. Although both sides claimed victory, in the end the Confederates, driven from the field, failed to destroy Grant's army and lost the momentum with which they had hoped to carry the war across the Tennessee and up the Ohio River.

The North, despite its heavy losses, paved the way for its domination of the Mississippi and the vertical split of the Confederacy.

Regardless of his later denials. Grant had been surprised at Shiloh. At the time he made no attempt to defend himself from widespread criticisms of his conduct, particularly the charge that he had been surprised because he was drunk. (Grant did, in fact, drink to excess on occasion and apparently had a problem in coping with alcohol. To his credit he seemed aware of this failing and, perhaps deliberately, chose as his adjutant and chief of staff a firm and stern tee-totaler, John A Rawlins, who kept an ever-watchful eye on him. Although undoubtedly there were lapses, certainly Grant never lost a battle because he was under the influence.) President Lincoln, responding to demands for Grant's dismissal, stuck by him, saying, 'I can't spare this man, he fights.' But Halleck, apparently convinced that Grant was too careless to be trusted, relegated him to a voiceless second-in-command that was so humiliating Grant decided to quit. Sherman, who came upon him packing up to leave for St Louis, talked him out of it.

Grant understood that the bloodiness and inconclusiveness of Shiloh changed the war and his perception of it. 'I gave up all idea of saving the Union except by complete conquest,' he wrote later in his *Memoirs*. More important, after Shiloh Grant began to realize that a new kind of war was evolving, war raged by the might and resources of one people upon the entire population and resources of another.

In July, after he was called to Washington to become general-in-chief of all union armies, Halleck assigned Grant the relatively inactive mission of protecting communications along the Mississippi, giving Buell, who had seen practically no fighting, the mission of taking the crucial Confederate rail center of Chattanooga. Stationed in Corinth, Grant studied maps and devised plans for taking Vicksburg, the Confederate 'Gibraltar of the West,' the capture of which would give the Union control of the Mississippi and of the last Confederate railroad leading east from the river, effectively cutting off supplies necesssary for the Southern war effort, and permitting Union armies and supplies to pass un-molested through the very center of the Confederacy. The Union now occupied Memphis, 400 miles above Vicksburg, and controlled the southern Mississippi up to Baton Rouge, Louisiana. In Washington, Lincoln remarked to Rear Admiral David Dixon Porter, 'See what a lot of land those fellows hold, of which Vicksburg is the key. . . . . The war cannot be brought to a close until that key is in our pocket.' Grant was given command of the Department of the Tennessee on 25 October 1962. One week later he started his campaign against Vicksburg.

Vicksburg was a fortress town on the first high land on the eastern bank of the Mississippi below Memphis, bristling with artillery and garrisoned by tens of thousands of Confederate soldiers. At this point in its course the Fathers of Waters wandered randomly for miles left and right and north and south through soft alluvial soil, cutting fresh channels through a land of low-lying islands, little peninsulas, and stagnant lakes to

Far left: Grant would record in his *Memoirs* that Shiloh changed his perception of the war, teaching him that restoration of the Union would demand 'complete conquest' of the Confederacy.

Near left: Union Admiral David Dixon Porter performed valuable service in supporting Grant's assault on Vicksburg.

Below: An 1865 lithograph entitled *Council of War* shows Lincoln conferring in the field with (from left) Admirals Porter and Farragut and Generals Sherman, Thomas, Grant and Sheridan.

create a swampy jungle forty miles across. With the town's fortifications and batteries rendering the river below all but impassable to Union ships, Vicksburg was approachable by land only from the east, through jealously guarded Confederate territory.

In November 1862 Grant marched on Vicksburg from Memphis with 30,000 men, sending Sherman down the river in a classic two-pronged advance. The Confederates, under General John C Pemberton, commander of Southern forces in Mississippi, halted this offensive on 20-25 December when Van Dorn's cavalry burned Grant's supply depot at Holly Springs, Mississippi, and Nathan Forrest's cavalry tore up his

railroad line of communications for sixty miles in Tennessee. Sherman was defeated on 27-29 December at Chickasaw Bluffs just north of Vicksburg, the Union suffering 1776 casualties to the South's 207. But instead of returning to Memphis and beginning a new attack, as convention and his subordinates agreed he should, Grant moved all of his forces to Young's Point, nearly opposite Vicksburg.

In the first months of 1863 Grant indulged in a series of experiments designed to concentrate Confederate attention on attacks from the north of Vicksburg. Known as the Bayou Expeditions – the principal projects were Duckport Canal, Lake Providence Expedition, Yazoo Pass Expedition, and Steele's Bayou Expedition – these attempts all centered on cutting waterways to get enough Union troop transports safely past Vicksburg's batteries for an attack from the south. As one bayou expedition after another failed, considerable Northern public opinion was mustered against Grant, who appeared to be throwing away money and lives and foundering in the watery bayous while Vicksburg stood as secure as ever. Lincoln, however, stuck by him. 'I rather like the man. I think I'll try him a little longer.'

Grant, who frequently visited his men in the field, appeared unconcerned. He seemed to have reached a new maturity and a fuller awareness of his own authority. Even Halleck, who, with the war stalled on all fronts, had become painfully aware that none of his other commanders were measuring up, expressed in his letters a new reliance on, and respect for, Grant.

Grant wrote his own orders whenever possible. They were sparing of verbiage and to the point. A typical order to Sherman, in its entirety, read, 'Take plenty of shovels and picks up to Rye Bend to clear the way.' According to one private soldier, 'He will ride along the long line of the army, apparently an indifferent observer, yet he sees and notices everything. He seems to know and remember every regiment, and in fact every cannon in his large army.'

As the last of the bayou ventures faded out, in late March, Grant, sure of himself, although perhaps not as yet completely aware that he was about to begin one of the boldest and most successful campaigns in military history, remarked, 'We are going through a campaign here such as has not been heard of on this continent before.' His plan comprised four operations to be executed in concert by his army, Admiral David Dixon Porter's fleet, Sherman's corps, and Colonel B H Grierson's cavalry. Grant, taking advantage of receding waters, would march his men down the west side of the Mississipppi to a point south of Vicksburg. Porter would run the dreadful Vicksburg batteries to meet Grant with supplies and transport to get his men across the river. Meanwhile, Sherman was to feint an attack at Haines's Bluff north of Vicksburg, then join Grant's main force downstream. As an additional diversion, Grierson, a former music teacher, was

Previous pages: Admiral Porter's fleet running the Confederate blockade of the Mississippi at Vicksburg, April 1863.

Below: The watery maze of bayous in the environs of Vicksburg proved impervious to Grant's efforts to use this roundabout way of taking the city.

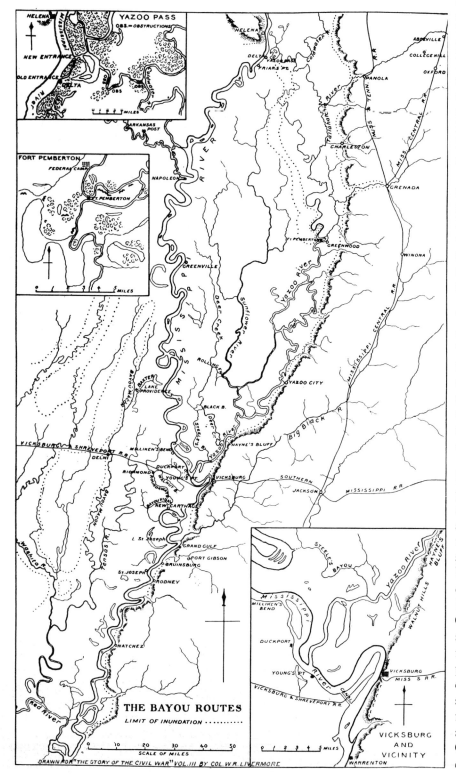

THE BAYOU ROUTES

LIMIT OF INUNDATION ....

DRAWN FOR "THE STORY OF THE CIVIL WAR" VOL. III BY COL. W.R. LIVERMORE

VICKSBURG AND VICINITY

Left: Grant was renowned for his horsemanship, which even his enemies admired.

Above: A Union recruiting poster offers incentives to enlistment.

Below: Forbidding bluffs along the Mississippi south of Vicksburg, at Port Hudson, Louisiana. The Union Army gathered on the Louisiana side of the river, at Hard Times Landing.

to move his 1700-man cavalry south from Tennessee through Mississippi, wreaking as much havoc as possible.

The final element in the equation was Washington. General John A McClernand had been planning a separate river expedition against Vicksburg, but Halleck put an end to it and placed McClernands's XIII Corps to cut a trail for his troops to follow from the Federal camp at Milliken's Bend south to New Carthage, Louisiana, below Vicksburg. On 16 April Porter ran the Vicksburg batteries, with the loss of only one ship and a few barges. On 22 April more transports and barges ran the gauntlet to join Grant's gathering army at Hard Times Landing, on the Louisiana side. Meanwhile, beginning at Haines's Bluff, Sherman kept moving his corps up and down the river until Confederate General Pemberton, in Vicksburg, became convinced a major attack was coming from that direction. Griersons's screening diversion, which left Tennessee on 17 April, one of the most brilliantly successful cavalry exploits of the war, confused Pemberton even more, who sent cavalry against Grierson and troops against Sherman.

Meanwhile Grant, who found stiff Confederate resistance at Grand Gulf, his chosen landing, maneuvered his way a little farther south and took his 20,000 men across the river at Bruinsburg on 30 April without a sign of opposition. On

1 May, after a hard day's fighting, he met, out-flanked, and brushed aside 8000 Confederate troops sent from Grand Gulf. His army, skirmishing constantly with enemy forces in their rear, continued to push northeast.

Thus far Grant's orders called for him to move south after crossing the river to join General Nathaniel P Banks for a joint assault aginst Port Hudson, then combine for a joint operation against Vicksburg. Banks, however, was completely taken up with the disastrous Red River Campaign. Whereupon, on his own, as was his custom, and against the advice of his subordinates, and in flagrant violation of his orders from Washington, Grant decided to cut away from his supply train and march against Jackson, 45 miles east of Vicksburg, where he was aware Confederate reinforcements were being gathered to oppose him under Joseph E Johnston, one of the ablest of the Confederate generals. His plan was to defeat Johnston at Jackson before moving on to Vicksburg, thereby avoiding the error of leaving enemy forces in the field that could come to Pemberton's assistance.

On 12 May 1863 Grant moved forward with an army of 44,000; Sherman had crossed to join him at Grand Gulf on 6 May. Free from their supply line, they moved quickly. In the first 18 days of May Grant's troops marched 200 miles, won four battles, and inflicted losses of 8000 men and 88 guns. This was possible because, as Grant well understood, his men were sons of pioneers, not professional soldiers schooled in a base-of-supply mentality, and were able to forage successfully

even before their three-days' rations gave out. The cost of the war was taken directly to the Southern civilians.

After sending a detachment to feint an attack on Vicksburg, Grant brushed aside light opposition south of Raymond and pushed on to Jackson, 15 miles to the northeast. The resistance he had met from Confederate John Gregg, as well as reports from Sherman and McClernand, confirmed his estimate of considerable Confederate force gathering at Jackson, where Johnston, with orders to take command of all Confederate forces in Mississippi, had arrived on the evening of 13 May. Aware of Grant's disposition between himself and Pemberton and backed by only 6000 men, Johnston realized he was too late. The Federals attacked at 10:00 AM on 14 May and entered Jackson by four that evening; that night Grant slept in the room Johnston had occupied the night before. Sherman, meantime, at Grant's request, set out to 'destroy everything public not needed by us.' Pemberton's – and Vicksburg's – railroad lifeline was turned into twisted metal.

Although Confederate President Jefferson Davis had ordered Pemberton to stay in Vicksburg and hold it at all costs, Johnston ordered Pemberton to cut Grant's supply line and join him with his army. Pemberton, who had ignored Johnston's previous orders to attack Grant's rear, spent 15 May looking for a supply line that did not exist, then turned east to join Johnston at Brownsville, his troops exhausted from much marching and no enemy. Grant, who had foreseen this course of Confederate events, left Sherman to complete the sack of Jackson and marched with McClernand and McPherson to meet Pemberton at Champion's Hill, a 75-foot knoll that afforded Pemberton an ideal position to block the roads to Vicksburg from the east.

The battle of Champion's Hill on 16 May was the hardest day's fighting of the campaign. The

Above: A view of the levee at Vicksburg, thronged with Mississippi steamboats. Once the river was reopened to shipping, the west was lost to the Confederacy; the South would soon be split again, along rail lines vital to the Confederate war effort.

Top left: A naval gun used in the capture of Port Hudson, five days after Vicksburg fell to Union forces.

IMPORTANT FROM AMERICA !!
Awful Slaughter at Vicksburg,
And Elsewhere,
The Bloody Conflict between the North & South
CONTINUED !

forces on each side were relatively equal in number and ability, and the fighting seesawed indecisively for hours. At last the Confederates withdrew to the Big Black River, in fairly good order, with Grant in pursuit. They had suffered 3851 casualties to the North's 2441.

Vicksburg was by now doomed, and Pemberton, as Johnston repeatedly ordered, ought to have evacuated the fortress and gone north to meet Johnston, thereby saving his army. Instead, he fell back toward Vicksburg, posting a rear guard before the Big Black River. In a one-hour fight on 17 May, 10,000 Federals pushed the 4000 defending Confederates into the river, capturing 1700. Federal pursuit halted when the Confederates burned the only bridge.

As the battle raged, a messenger finally reached Grant with a message from Halleck ordering him to retire immediately to Grand Gulf and then to proceed in support of Banks at Port Hudson. Simultaneously, Grant heard a cheer indicating a successful charge. Telling the messenger, 'See that charge! I think it's too late to abandon this campaign,' he jumped on his horse and rode toward the action. His reputation was on the ascendant again.

That night 30,000 weary Confederate soldiers, 'wan, hollow-eyed, ragged, footsore,' limped into Vicksburg, threatening to swamp the city. The next day, 18 May, Grant seized the high ground overlooking the Yazoo River north of the city, gaining a base for supplies and reinforcements that would enable Federal forces to swell to 71,000 within a month. While his troops crossed a new bridge over the Big Black, he sent a detachment to forestall any rescue attempt by Johnston. Johnston had again advised Pemberton to abandon Vicksburg, but even if he had wanted to, it was too late for Pemberton to move. He was trapped in Vicksburg, and Johnston was unable to come to his rescue.

But Vicksburg itself was still to be captured. In addition to naturally broken ground, which in itself presented a formidable obstacle to any attacker, elaborate fortifications had been built up around Vicksburg. Seven months in the

Above: A Dublin newspaper reports on the American Civil War, in which thousands of Irish immigrants were involved. Some 50,000 Irish immigrants arrived in New York between January and June of 1863 alone.

Above: Vicksburg was a good place to defend and a dangerous one to attack. The Confederates had spent seven months fortifying the site, with nine forts as strong points in a line nine miles long.

Confederate General John C Pemberton, Vicksburg's commander, surrendered his garrison 4 July 1863; Grant agreed to parole the Confederate defenders rather than imprison them.

making, they comprised a line nine miles long with nine forts as strong points on the principal avenues of approach. Grant wanted to avoid a long siege, for which he would have to draw troops from Memphis, and was anxious to take the city before Johnston could assemble a stronger force. He also firmly believed Pemberton's men were demoralized by their recent defeats. But he clearly underestimated Confederate strength and will to resist. He ordered a frontal attack on 19 May, which met savage resistance and made no headway. As usual, Grant was to be

found where the fighting was heaviest. Some felt he actually enjoyed being under heavy fire, as a man might enjoy being out in the rain on a hot day.

On 22 May Grant, still unwilling to countenance a lengthy siege, mounted another frontal attack. After an hour and a half of heavy fighting he was ready to call a halt, but misleading reports from McClernand, who claimed he was breaking through, induced him to order a final, fruitless assault. The result was 3200 Union casualties for the two days; 13,000 Confederate effectives had succeeded in turning back 35,000 Federals.

Vicksburg, a thriving commercial center of 4500 before the war, with strong ties to the North (its citizens had opposed secession in 1860), now became the only sizeable American city ever to endure total siege. Grant gradually extended fifteen miles of lines around Vicksburg, ringing it so tightly that, according to one Confederate soldier, 'a cat could not have crept out of Vicksburg.' Under the constant shelling of Porter's fleet and Grant's army, the citizens went underground, digging caves into the hillsides. By late June mule and peas headed the Vicksburg bill of fare; after most of the army's mules had been consumed, soldiers ate fried rat.

At the beginning of July at least 10,000 Confederate soldiers were unfit for service. Vicksburg's civilians fared no better. On 3 July white flags appeared on the ramparts of Vicksburg, and Pemberton, who, as a lieutenant in Mexico, had once carried their mutual general's compliments to Grant for his creative use of a church belfry as an artillery post, came out to discuss terms. When Pemberton refused Grant's offer of unconditional surrender, Grant agreed to the paroling of Pemberton's army. Sending prisoners north to prison camps would tie up his own army and transportation system, and he also felt that the sudden influx of 30,000 refugees would put a strain on the Confederate economy.

Grant rode into Vicksburg to take surrender from Pemberton on 4 July 1863. Pemberton offered him his sword with belt and revolver attached; Grant responded, 'Retain your side arms, General.' At three o'clock that afternoon 30,000 hungry Confederates filed out of Vicksburg to stack their arms; in all, 60,000 small arms and 172 cannon were seized. The Union troops watched in silence. Grant had forbidden any demonstration of triumph by his troops, as he would do at future victories.

Grant had achieved one of the most brilliant successes in military history, and he had done it more on maneuver than on fighting. The victory demonstrated his gift for long-range strategic planning and for utilizing the superior manpower and industrial strength of the North. Including casualties, 40,000 Confederate troops were now out of the war; Federal casualties for the campaign were about 10,000. Vicksburg would not again officially celebrate Independence Day until 1945.

The battle of Gettysburg, which had ended the day before Vicksburg's capitulation, was a great victory for the North; but the Union victory at Vicksburg, the greatest surrender ever seen on the American continent, was one of the most decisive in the war. It freed Grant's army for further efforts, opened the Mississippi to the North for trade with the rest of the world, eliminated a major Confederate army from the conflict, and cut the Confederacy in half. With the fall of Vicksburg, the Confederacy had, in effect, lost the war.

Lincoln nominated Grant major general in the regular army, a nomination promptly seconded by a grateful Congress. In October he was given command of all troops between the Mississippi and the Alleghenies (with the exception of Banks's in Mississippi), and called upon by Lincoln to rescue the Union forces pinned down by Confederate General Braxton Bragg at the Confederate rail and industrial center of Chattanooga – after Vicksburg, the most strategically important Southern town. To the demoralized Union commander General William S Rosecrans and his half-starved troops, languishing in their desperate besieged state, the man who had come to save them, the victor of Fort Henry, Fort Donelson, Shiloh, and Vicksburg, appeared inattentive and disreputable. Instead of a swaggering hero, they beheld a silent, 'short, round-shouldered man, in a very tarnished uniform.'

Grant acted quickly, replacing the disintegrating Rosecrans with Major General George Henry Thomas. He ordered Sherman to march

east, and opened a 'cracker line' to bring in desperately needed food and clothing for the garrison; reinforcements from the Army of the Potomac were moved west by rail. Less than a month after his arrival on a scene of impending Union disaster, Grant was prepared to take the offensive. On 25 November his vindictive Federals, having already achieved their objective, stormed Missionary Ridge without orders and chased a demoralized Bragg and his Confederate Army of Tennessee back to Georgia.

In Washington Grant received the personal thanks of President Lincoln and a gold medal voted by Congress. In March 1864 he was promoted to the rank of lieutnant general and given command of all the armies of the United States. He now turned his attention to winning the war, and drew up the first comprehensive plan of action since the beginning of the war for the Union armies as a whole. Three years before he had been a clerk in his brothers' leather goods store. Now he was in a position to carry out the grandest strategy an American general had ever conceived: engage all his troops simultaneously to cut the Confederacy into fragments by preventing its armies from reinforcing each other and destroy them by pursuing them relentlessly and pounding them to pieces.

Above: French artist Louis Mercier made this etching of *Le Général Grant* soon after the Civil War. European countries took a keen interest in the conflict, reporting on it regularly in their news media and in some cases sending observers to the scenes of battle for prolonged periods.

GEORGE HENRY THOMAS

Chickamauga
Chattanooga

Command post at the Battle
of Chattanooga, 23-25
November 1863.

In the days after Gettysburg the Union had but one goal: complete victory. As minor skirmishes continued between Lee's retreating and Meade's tardily pursuing forces, matters were coming to a head in the western war theater. There, the often difficult General William Starkie Rosecrans was moving the Union Army of the Cumberland toward Chattanooga, in concert with General Ambrose Burnside. Their aim: to capture Chattanooga with its vital rail lines, and to crush the Confederate army between them, using their forces as mighty pincers.

First, the Tennessee River had to be crossed; second, General Braxton Bragg's Confederate army had to be found; third, the Rebels had to be forced to stand and fight. Rosecrans crossed the main force of his army between the first and fourth of September, but when Bragg slipped out of Chattanooga with 65,000 men on 8 September 1863, Rosecrans became convinced of the wisdom of splitting his forces into three main bodies. One, under Major General Thomas Crittenden, would head north for Chattanooga, while George Henry Thomas held the center and Alexander McCook headed south. The Union strategy was clear: find Bragg wherever he was. Bragg's strategy was no less clear: isolate and defeat the three arms of Rosecrans' forces one by one. The issue was to be decided on 19 and 20 September 1863 at the Battle of Chickamauga, seven miles southeast of Chattanooga on the Chickamauga Creek, a tributary of the Tennessee River. This was not the first battle to be fought along the Chickamauga, which the Cherokee Indians had named 'River of Death' because of the number of skirmishes thereabout between warring Indian tribes.

By 12 September Rosecrans had realized, tardily, that Bragg was not retreating but feinting. By 18 September Rosecrans and Bragg were deployed along the Chickamauga Creek, scrambling for defensible positions in the thickly wooded and rugged terrain. Not only were the Union forces not sure of Bragg's precise position, they were not sure where their own battalions were. Uncertainty prevented the opposing forces from joining battle on the 18th, but on the 19th troops commanded by the man who would soon be known as 'The Rock of Chickamauga' – George Henry Thomas – would fire the first shots of the bloody two-day battle in which casualties would run as high as 28 percent on both sides, leaving a total of 37,129 dead or wounded.

Thomas was an unlikely man to initiate the battle: his nickname until then, 'Old Slow Trot,' went back to his West Point days. Whenever Thomas drilled the cavalry cadets, he would urge them not to exceed a 'slow trot.' Later, the nickname stuck because of his caution and deliberation in action. Grant himself was rumored to have said of Thomas that he was 'Too slow to fight, and too brave to run away.'

George Henry Thomas had followed the usual military career of his day: West Point, the Florida

war against the Seminoles, and service in the Mexican War. When the Civil War broke out, Thomas, who had been born in Southampton County, Virginia, in 1816, took his time deciding whether to serve with his native Virginia or with the Union. There were those (enemies on both the Confederate and Union sides) who alleged that Thomas chose the Union only because he perceived his chances of advancement to be greater there. The rumor was likewise whispered about that Thomas was unduly under the influence of his Northern wife.

Be that as it may, as late as January 1861, when Thomas visited his sister in Virginia, he seems to have let his Southern relatives think he would

Above: An etching that appeared in *Harper's Weekly,* captioned 'Thomas's Men Repulsing the Charges of the Rebels' at the Battle of Chickamauga.

Right: General Ambrose Everett Burnside, by capturing and holding Knoxville, aided the Union victory at Chattanooga in September 1863.

stand with Virginia. Indeed, shortly after that visit he wrote to the head of the Virginia Military Institute asking information on an advertised vacancy as commandant of cadets and instructor of tactics. As he wrote to the superintendent, 'I will be under obligations if you will inform me what salary and allowances pertain to the situation, as from present appearances I feel it will soon be necessary for me to be looking up some means of support.'

Whatever Thomas's doubts about whether to stand with his native Virginia or the Union, they seem to have been resolved once war broke out: he became a colonel in the Federal forces on 3 May 1861. By November he was in command of

Lieutenant Van Pelt defends his battery at the Battle of Chickamauga, September 1863.

the First Division of the Army of the Ohio and won a small, but significant, victory at Mill Springs, Kentucky, where he pushed forward across the Cumberland River in pursuit of Confederate soldiers under the command of General Felix Zollicoffer. The skirmish was brief, but Thomas netted the North considerable booty: 10 cannon, 100 wagons, 1000 horses, and numerous transport boats. As a result of his victory at Mill Springs Thomas was promoted to brigadier general. Ironically, Thomas forgot on the battlefield – it was his first command – to ask for formal surrender from the Rebel leader. When one of his men, Colonel Speed S Fry, questioned him afterward about the omission, Thomas replied, 'Hang it all, Fry, I never once thought of it!'

Despite the victory at Mill Springs, Thomas's hesitation at the beginning of the war was remembered, and may have made him all the more determined at Chickamauga to prove his loyalty and worth. On the morning of 19 September Thomas ordered his cavalry to reconnoiter, in an attempt to pinpoint the exact location of the Confederate forces. When Union cavalry encountered some dismounted Confederate cavalry, fighting broke out, and ultimately involved most of the forces on both sides. The fighting was fierce and confused in the thickets along the Chickamauga, and particularly fierce on the left Federal flank, where Thomas was stationed.

Had the Confederate General Bragg but known it, the Union lines were stretched dangerously thin – there was a gap of several miles between Crittenden and Thomas's units. Only Bragg's inability to locate this gap prevented the South from being presented with a ready-made

opportunity to pierce the Union lines and attack from the rear. By nightfall, when the fighting had died away, casualties were high, but little had been gained by either side.

That night Thomas met with the rest of Rosecrans's senior officers at staff headquarters at the Widow Glenn's house, south of the main battle line. Each corps commander gave his report and was asked his opinion as to the morrow. Thomas, exhausted, dozed off from time to time, awaking periodically to urge, 'Strengthen the left!' It was not until almost two in the morning that Thomas regained his unit, and before dawn he was directing the erection of defensive breastworks. After the war, when a group of Southern and Northern former officers revisited the battlefield, one Southerner gestured to the remains of Thomas's log and rail breastworks and remarked,

Top: The wounding of General Hood at the Battle of Chickamauga.

Above: On the road to Chickamauga, both armies left destruction of land and property behind.

Opposite: General William Starkie Rosecrans (1819-1898). Although Rosecrans became a hero after the battle at Stone's River, Tennessee, his next conflict with Bragg at Chickamauga was a disaster.

'Only for this little work, we would have swept you from the field before noon.' It was a fitting tribute to the meticulous skills of the man who was fond of saying, 'The fate of a battle may depend on a buckle.'

The fate of that battle on 20 September depended on more than a buckle, on more than Thomas's fastidious soldiering; it depended on his dogged determination and courage. All that morning Thomas continued to be concerned about whether his line was sufficiently strong and to ask Rosecrans for reinforcements. Yet, when fighting broke out, Thomas held the left Federal line in fierce fighting from 9:00 to 11:00 AM. At that point, by a terrible mishap, perhaps caused in part by the thick fog that obscured the terrain, Union General Thomas Wood drew back, creating a gap in the Union lines. This day the Union forces were not as fortunate as they had been on the previous day in similar circumstances: this time Confederate General Longstreet found the gap in the Union lines and charged, with his full force, through the gap, routing the Union forces. As Thomas retreated with his men to Snodgrass Hill, Rosecrans retreated altogether (some would say fled) toward Chattanooga, with most of the Union forces following.

As one soldier later recalled, Thomas's 'calm, invincible will never bent.' The situation, despite Thomas's resolve and his men's valor, was desperate until, at 3:30 PM, General James B Steedman arrived with reinforcements. As important as the fresh soldiers was the supply of ammunition they brought with them. Now Thomas could clearly hold out and pick his moment to retreat and rejoin Rosecrans. This he did, withdrawing from Snodgrass Hill around

6:00 PM; shortly thereafter, the Confederates took the hill, but the moment was without joy.

Chickamauga had been a disastrous defeat for the Union forces, and a personally humiliating defeat for the commander, General Rosecrans. Nonetheless, it was a great personal victory for Thomas, whose actions had prevented the defeat from becoming absolute. Now the Union troops could regroup and turn their attention to their original goal: Chattanooga, where Federal soldiers would storm Confederate lines with a new battle cry: 'Chickamauga!' Forever after, Thomas would be known as 'The Rock of Chickamauga' because he had stood like a rock on the battlefield against fearful odds. 'Old Slow Trot' had a new, and glorious, nickname.

After Chickamauga Rosecrans and the Union forces holed up at Chattanooga while Bragg laid siege to the battered Federals. By October Rosecrans had to put both men and animals on starvation rations. The Confederate forces held the main railroad, hence the supply lines into Chattanooga, and only the arrival on 30 October of a steamboat full of provisions staved off utter starvation. Not surprisingly Rosecrans was relieved of his command on 23 October, and Thomas was appointed Commander of the Army of the Cumberland. At the same time, Grant was named head of the new military division of the Mississippi. The situation remained perilous for the Union forces; in early November Thomas was unable to accept Grant's order to move out his troops, as his artillery horses were too weak to pull the heavy guns.

It was unfortunate that, in circumstances already trying, Thomas's characteristic reserve (some said aloofness) had distinctly *not* endeared him to his new commander, Ulysses S Grant. In

Above: The Confederate line of battle in the Chickamauga woods.

Opposite top: Fierce fighting in the Battle of Lookout Mountain.

Opposite bottom: Fog and smoke made visibility slight for both sides, obscuring the positions of friend and foe alike.

fact, when Grant arrived at Thomas's headquarters in Chattanooga on 23 October, muddy,
wet, and exhausted from a particularly arduous
journey through the Confederate lines, Thomas
let his new commanding officer sit dripping
miserably by the fire. Finally, another officer
suggested that Grant might benefit from some dry
clothes, and suggested further that Thomas might
have some to offer. Thomas's behavior, callous if
not almost churlish, is all the more difficult to
fathom as Grant's first act on arriving had been to
present a letter of commendation from Secretary
of War Stanton. 'You stood like a rock,' Stanton
had written to Thomas, 'and that stand gives you
fame which will grow brighter as the ages go by.
You will be rewarded by the country and the
Department.'

Chattanooga was not the first time Grant and
Thomas had ruffled each other's fur. The previous year, in the battle at Corinth, Mississippi,
General Henry W Halleck had slighted Grant by
promoting Thomas. Both Grant and Thomas

Left: General Thomas's charge near Orchard Knob in the Battle of Chattanooga.

Above: A typical Confederate artillery gunner, resting on his weapon.

were aware of the awkwardness, with Grant immediately angry, and Thomas's initial pride in the promotion swiftly dimmed by his realization that Halleck had used him to humiliate Grant. Nor would Chattanooga be the last time these two difficult men – the often irascible Grant and the habitually stiff Thomas – would wear on each other's nerves. The following year, at Petersburg, Grant would be infuriated by Thomas's slowness and obstinacy.

If the animosity between Grant and Thomas was clear in the days before Chattanooga, little else was. Inconclusive skirmishing went on from Grant's arrival on 23 October until finally, on 23 November, the three-day Battle of Chattanooga was joined. Grant's plan was to hit the Confederates with a three-pronged attack, first to the north, then straight through the center, all the while deploying some troops to the south in an attempt to mislead the enemy as to where the main Federal attack would come. In addition, Grant determined on a bold ploy to lull the Rebel forces into a false sense of security: he would stage a mock drill with the 25,000 men of the Army of the Cumberland.

At dawn Union artillery broke the silence, with the Confederate guns answering; the firing continued until midday, then died away. At about 1:30 PM Thomas, as ordered by Grant, moved his troops toward the Confederate lines, flags flying and drummer boys drumming, as bugles sounded the call to battle. Grant's ploy worked: the Confederate forces thought they were watching not an attack but a parade drill. Suddenly, the full force of the Army of the Cumberland wheeled, stormed the Rebel positions, and overwhelmed them. The surprise was so great, and the assault so vigorous, that the Confederates yielded the day early and retreated, leaving Union forces in possession of Orchard Knob, a strategic lookout point between Chattanooga itself and Missionary Ridge, where the Confederate troops were arrayed.

Above: In the Civil War troops were often brought to the battlefield by train. Here the Nashville and Chattanooga Railroad transports troops from Lookout Mountain.

Opposite: Portraits of the Union generals.

That night, under cover of darkness, a well-planned Union maneuver took place, as General Sherman moved 8000 men across the Tennessee River in a flotilla of more than 116 boats, which had been hidden for days among the reeds along the river bank. At dawn, when General Bragg looked out from his command post on Missionary Ridge, he saw Sherman's reinforcements in place. It was not a good omen for the Confederates.

The next day saw the Battle of Lookout Mountain, known poetically as the 'Battle Above the Clouds' because of thick ground fog that obscured all but the highest plateau of the 1110-foot mountain. At dawn Lookout Mountain was held by the Confederate forces; by dusk the Federals held the eminence. Sherman's reinforcements carried the day, although at nightfall Sherman discovered that due to the limited visibility he had not taken the north flank of Missionary Ridge, as he thought, but a small hill nearby. To make matters worse, Sherman was separated from his goal by the treacherous ravine between the hillock and Missionary Ridge.

The next day's action was concentrated pri-marily on Missionary Ridge, and Thomas played a critical, albeit inadvertent, role in the battle. The day began with fierce, if inconclusive fighting, which lasted until midday and then died down as both sides gathered their strength for the final assault. Grant's orders to Thomas were bold, particularly since Thomas was known best for his defensive, not his offensive, capabilities. Now Grant ordered Thomas to direct the Army of the Cumberland in a frontal assault on Missionary Ridge. Anticipating fierce enemy crossfire, Grant further ordered that the assault forces stop and regroup halfway up the ridge.

These were the orders Grant gave and Thomas relayed to the Army of the Cumberland. But the battle was about to pass from the hands of the commanders into the grasp of the men and become a true 'soldiers battle.' The raking crossfire from above, which Grant had anticipated and which had caused him to order the attacking force to stop and regroup at the halfway point, was so fierce that the men realized they would be sitting ducks if they paused for a moment. On they went, up the ridge, four divisions strong, while Grant asked Thomas, 'Who ordered those

MAJ. GEN. J. M. SCHOFIELD.

MAJ. GEN. G. H. THOMAS.

MAJ. GEN. J. B. McPHERSON.

MAJ. GEN. H. W. SLOCUM.

MAJ. GEN. W. T. SHERMAN.

MAJ. GEN. O. O. HOWARD.

MAJ. GEN. A. H. TERRY.

MAJ. GEN. W. S. ROSECRANS.

MAJ. GEN. E. R. S. CANBY.

Eng^d by H. B. Hall Jr.

UNION GENERALS.

ENGRAVED EXPRESSLY FOR ABBOTTS CIVIL WAR

men to attack?' and Thomas replied laconically that it appeared that the men had issued their own orders.

Later, when the Union forces held Missionary Ridge, there were those who called the assault – up a heavily defended hill under raking fire – a miracle, and those who called it an accident, even a miraculous accident. Thomas had more than met Grant's orders that Chattanooga be held 'at all hazards.' It had been a close thing, but now the Union was no longer under siege at Chattanooga; now the Union had secured Chattanooga and had taken 2000 prisoners and captured 37 pieces of heavy artillery. Now, as Bragg was forced to withdraw south toward Ringgold, Georgia, Sherman and Thomas were in pursuit, eager to force the shattered Confederate army to stand and fight.

After Chattanooga, Sherman, and with him Thomas and the Army of the Cumberland, embarked on what came to be known as the Atlanta Campaign. Thomas's men were among the first to enter Atlanta, beginning on 2 September 1864. After the fall of Atlanta, Thomas (by now in Nashville, Tennessee) was formally detached from Sherman's main force on 26 October. Sherman would march south, toward the sea, while Thomas watched to learn whether the Confederates under General John B Hood followed or attacked strategic Union-held cities such as Nashville. Thomas had 35,000 men of his own, and was soon to receive reinforcements of almost that many again, drawn from wherever there were men to spare. The situation was complicated by the fact that neighboring Kentucky was in a state of considerable unrest, which made it risky to move too many troops out of Kentucky and into Tennessee. Furthermore, some of Thomas's new recruits were untrained and some, indeed, were criminals, released from prison in the Union's desperate attempt to get as many men in uniform as possible.

With this untried army, Thomas was to defend some 500 miles of territory, from the Cumberland Gap to Paducah, along the Tennessee River, against any Confederate attack. To assist him, Thomas ordered General John Schofield to serve as a mobile defense unit, ready to move quickly to check Hood. First, however, both Thomas and Schofield had to wait and watch. Would Hood head south after Sherman or attempt to take Chattanooga or Nashville? On 27 November Thomas concluded from the intelligence he was receiving that Hood was heading for Nashville. He at once ordered Schofield to contain Hood if possible and defend the roads into Nashville from the south. Oddly, General Hood allowed Schofield's men to slip past his troops at Columbia, some 40 miles south of Nashville, and to take up a strong position at Franklin, 15 miles south of Nashville on the Duck River.

The charge of the Third Brigade, First Division, Sixteenth Corps, at the Battle of Nashville, Tennessee.

The Nashville and
Chattanooga Railroad
Bridge in ruins.

On 29 November it was clear to Thomas that Hood was moving again; between him and Nashville stood Schofield. With the Duck River to his back and no boats or pontoon barges at hand, Schofield had but one choice: to stand and fight. This he did, stopping Hood's men in their tracks as they advanced in what later seemed almost a suicide attack. As one Southern survivor of the battle at Franklin recalled later, 'the enemy's line was crossed in one or two places, but no man who went over was ever to return.' In all, 6500 Confederate soldiers were killed at Franklin, only 100 less than died in the three days of fighting at Chattanooga.

After the victory at Franklin, Thomas had the luxury of a little time, and could afford to draw his men together and wait for the best moment to strike against Hood's battered army. As usual, Ulysses S Grant thought that Thomas was waiting too long. In early December Grant ordered Thomas to pursue and attack Hood's army. Thomas declined, and Grant fumed. On 9 December Grant felt that he could wait no longer: he ordered Thomas to hand over his command to the victor of Franklin, Schofield. Finally, on 15 December, furious and wondering if Thomas would ever step down or fight, Grant sent General John A Logan to replace Thomas. Perhaps, Grant thought, Logan could get through where telegrams had failed. Ironically, as Logan set off to relieve Thomas of his command, Thomas finally struck Hood with his full force. The Battle of Nashville had begun.

It was a characteristic Thomas battle. First,

Thomas had waited (enraging Grant, and prompting fresh rumors of his incompetence and dilatoriness), checked every buckle, and then attacked with overwhelming force. To be sure, Thomas has certain advantages: his men held Nashville, Hood's were bivouacked outside the city; he could retreat into Nashville, Hood must take the city from the Union forces. Thomas's army was at full strength, while Hood's was badly depleted. Finally, Thomas's cavalry was on hand, Hood's cavalry was away at Murfreesboro. Under the daylong Union attack, Hood's lines were first constricted and then forced to retreat. At nightfall Thomas was convinced that Hood would retreat under cover of night. Hood did not so oblige him. He stood and fought a second day on the plain outside Nashville beneath the Brentwood Hills. Again Thomas threw his main strength at the Confederate left flank, in the hope of breaking the line and encircling the enemy. This time Thomas was successful, the Confederate lines broke utterly, and the remnants of Hood's army fled south back toward Franklin.

Thomas had won a decisive victory; it had broken the fighting power of the Army of the Tennessee once and for all. Indeed, Nashville was one of the decisive battles of the war in that it dealt a death blow to Southern hopes to regroup and carry on the conflict in the west. Thomas recognized the battle's significance by sending his only known message of victory to his wife, a telegram stating, 'We have whipped the enemy, taken many prisoners and considerable artillery,'

Hood was virtually destroyed and on the run, Thomas was vindicated. Grant recognized this, and sent Thomas a telegram of congratulations while quietly recalling General Logan, who had not reached Thomas's headquarters.

For the next 30 days Thomas pursued Hood, through appalling weather conditions, in which it took 12 hours for horses to pull a wagon six miles. When it was done, Thomas had virtually annihilated Hood's army.

Nashville was Thomas's last major engagement during the war; the next months, until the war's end, were spent in mopping-up operations. When peace came, Thomas remained on active duty, and served as commander of the Military Division of the Pacific. He died of apoplexy in San Francisco in 1869. Although the least charismatic of the Union generals, Thomas had been urged to stand for the Presidency after the war, an honor he left to his old comrade-in-arms Ulysses S Grant.

Thomas was, for all his reserve, a man of contradictions, on the one hand capable of sending for his army cot when a hotel bed struck him as too sybaritic, on the other hand alternately amusing and appalling his officers by his habit of dining on the march with silver tableware and a uniformed black major domo. He was punctilious to a fault, once sending out invitations to dinner marked RSVP to his staff in the midst of a campaign.

One friend described Thomas's eyes as 'cold gray to his enemies, but warm deep blue to his friends': it would appear that Grant most often saw the cold, gray eyes, but others recalled a 'smile of welcome [both] pleasant and most cordial.' Perhaps most illuminating is the remark Thomas made of himself: 'I have taken a great deal of pains to educate myself not to feel.' And yet it was this same man, educated not to feel, who, after the Battle of Chattanooga, toured the battlefield to pick the site for a cemetery for the fallen. When a staff officer asked whether there should be two cemeteries, one for the Union and one for the Confederate dead, Thomas replied, 'No, mix 'em up. I've had enough of states' rights.' Despite his determination 'not to feel,' he was perhaps thinking about his native state, Virginia, and perceived regretfully the destructive and divisive effects on it of the Civil War.

Top: A rare photograph of the Union line at Nashville.

Above: Troops gather for an informal service at the makeshift Grant Bethesda Church.

NATHAN BEDFORD FORREST

Fort Donelson
Fort Pillow
Brice's Cross Roads

The Battle of Fort
Donelson, Tennessee,
16 February 1862.

On the whole the Civil War was directed by men who had been trained for the job: West Pointers who together had fought Mexicans and Indians before being set against one another. The pre-eminent exception to this rule was Nathan Bedford Forrest. By no means the only amateur to lead men during the war, he was the only one who became a soldier of genius.

A photograph shows the forty-year-old Forrest just before he enlisted. Handsomely groomed and turned out, he looks very much what he was at the time, a successful businessman and gentleman – a millionaire, in fact. Only, perhaps, in the unflinching gaze and adamant set of his jaw can one discern the power that was soon to be unleashed.

Where Forrest's genius for cavalry tactics came from no one can say. He had more than an ability to size up a battle and respond to it with cunning and calculated ferocity. He also arrived early at a new understanding of the role of cavalry, an understanding to which his compatriots and his opponents came only belatedly: Forrest's riders fought dragoon-style, riding to battle and dismounting to fight. This idea of highly mobile striking power was to bear fruit from that point on in warfare, from the campaigns of Philip Sheridan to the mechanized mobility of Germany in World

Confederates under Nathan B Forrest storm Fort Pillow in April 1864. Colonel McCulloch commanded the left wing, seen here.

War II and beyond to the 'air cavalry' of Vietnam.

Forrest, by all reports, was in ordinary life a gentle and quiet-spoken man of unusually temperate habits – he drank little and, even more exceptional for the time, neither smoked nor chewed tobacco. His only vice was his lightning-bolt temper, which got him in trouble time and again but never seemed to damage his effectiveness on the battlefiled. The old legend that he was nearly illiterate is untrue. Though he had no formal schooling to speak of, he was expert in mathematics and succinct in his speech. It was his spelling that was ungovernable: he spelled as he fought, by instinct. (A subordinate's third request for a transfer brought the written reply, 'I have tole you twict goddamit No!')

His Southern drawl gained him his most famous quote, which was based on something he cited as his prime rule of strategy. Whipped up by newspapers into something more rusticated than his actual speech, that rule was: 'Git thar fustest with the mostest.' However he really put it, that little maxim could replace volumes of military theory. And he followed it. In action, Forrest rarely stood and waited but responded to threat with attack, showing a remarkable ability to maneuver his usually outnumbered forces to gain local superiority and win the field.

Below: A battle-torn Confederate flag.

Bottom: A Union cavalryman, outfitted as the Confederates could not afford to be.

In his personal life always the courtly Southern gentleman, in battle he was fierce and profane and seemingly capable of any violence, though he never lost control of himself and of events. He was usually to be found somewhere in the front line, perhaps more often there than any general of his caliber on either side. It is astonishing that he survived the war; he was wounded four times and had 20 horses shot from under him, meanwhile accounting for some 30 enemy casualties in hand-to-hand fighting. His men believed in Old Bedford with that wholehearted, headlong faith that in all wars at all times is the primary formula for victory.

Forrest was born to a blacksmith's family in Bedford County, Tennessee, on 13 July 1821. His father died when he was 16, and thereafter he assumed responsibility for his large family. At first Forrest farmed, then moved on to trading in livestock and then to trading in men: he was a slave dealer in Mississippi. (This background marked him for the rest of his life. Despite their defense of the institution of slavery, Southerners looked down on actual slave-trading and those who were engaged in it.) By 1845 Forrest had prospered enough to own two cotton plantations and many slaves. Moving to Memphis, Tennessee, in 1849, he became known about town as a prominent businessman. Perhaps the only hint of his future performance under duress came in 1857, when he faced down a lynch mob and cut the rope from the victim's neck.

Forrest enlisted for service as a private in the Confederate army in June 1861. After service in a company of mounted rifles, he gained from the Tennessee governor permission to raise his own battalion of volunteer cavalry. Equipping his men out of his own pocket, he took command as a lieutenant colonel. It was not long before his men saw battle and Forrest discovered his talents for the science of mayhem.

His battalion ran into a Federal scouting expedition at Sacramento, Kentucky, on 26 December 1861. Faced with superior forces, Forrest pulled back his center and drew the enemy forward, the Northerners assuming he was retreating. The pursuing Yankees then discovered themselves attacked on both flanks. As the enemy line faltered, Forrest stood his six feet two in the stirrups, roared 'Charge!' and led his men forward. Several hours and 25 miles later the enemy was in full rout. The Forrest style had emerged full-blown in his first engagement.

February 1862 found Forrest in the command of General Gideon J Pillow and Simon B Buckner at Fort Donelson, a Rebel stronghold dominating a bluff over the Cumberland River in middle Tennessee. Forrest and his men were ordered to make a reconnaissance of an approaching Federal army. The commander of these Yankees happened to be an up-and-coming bluecoat general named Ulysses S Grant, who had just won himself a handsome victory at Fort Henry.

Making contact on 11 February, Forrest found

the enemy advancing in force, enough so as to push him back whence he came after vigorous skirmishing. Next day, as the weather turned to snow and below-zero temperatures, General Pillow called everything he had into the fort, about 19,000 men in all. That night soldiers on both sides had a miserable time of it, the wounded lying unprotected in the vicious cold. Next day Pillow finished his concentration as Grant's 27,000 Federals enveloped the garrison. Then, when he was ready and able to make a stand, Pillow succumbed to fears of enemy numbers and of the weather and decided his troops would try to fight their way out and make a run for it. On the 14th Union gunboats arrived on the river and opened up on Donelson, but the Confederate artillery, though heavily outgunned, bested the Federal flotilla and sent it back upriver. That night Pillow decided that his forces, with Forrest as the spearhead, would strike on the left and open up the way to Charlotte and Nashville.

On the 15th Forrest led his men out into the

ungodly cold at 5:30 AM. After several hours of hard fighting in dense undergrowth, they had captured six enemy cannon. He was then sent to the right and led a charge that captured three more cannon. Forrest had soon had his first three horses shot from under him and had opened three roads of escape.

Then Pillow faltered again, calling off the offensive in the afternoon. In a midnight council of war, over Forrest's protests, Pillow and Buckner decided to surrender. Saying 'I cannot and will not surrender my command or myself,' Forrest got permission to lead any volunteers out; 1500 men responded, most from his battalion. During the night Forrest led them though Union lines to safety without seeing a Yankee or firing a shot. Next day the fort asked for terms and Grant's reply was a curt demand for 'immediate and unconditional surrender.' While Forrest rode to Nashville with his escapees, Grant swallowed the rest of the garrison whole. Forts Henry and Donelson were the first decisive Union victories

of the war, and the North erupted in celebration. From Fort Donelson both Grant and Forrest emerged into the public eye as men to be reckoned with. For Forrest it was to be one of his few losing encounters.

By April his battalion had been increased to a regiment, and Forrest joined with General Albert S Johnston's army in attacking Grant at Pittsburg Landing in southwest Tennessee. Before dawn on 6 April the Confederates began the devastating battle of Shiloh, driving the surprised Federals very nearly into the Tennessee River. Johnston was killed in the day's fighting. During the night Forrest entreated P G T Beauregard, the new commander, to attack at dawn on the morrow. Instead, it was Grant who attacked early, sending the Confederates into retreat after a murderous day of charge and countercharge around the little Shiloh church. It fell to Forrest to guard the Confederate rear against the troops of an adversary he was not to forget or ignore, William Tecumseh Sherman. As his men slowed the

Yankee advance with spattering blasts from shot-guns, Forrest as usual in the thick of the fighting, he took a bullet in the side that lodged near his spine. Doctors pronounced the wound fatal, but in three weeks Forrest was in the saddle again.

With the endorsement of General Braxton Bragg, Richmond set Forrest to raiding Union communications. He was to pursue the guerrilla's trade for most of the remainder of the war, often operating behind enemy lines. At that point Richmond's trust in this new man showed good sense. Over the long run, however, Confederate leaders were to prove themselves obtuse in failing to trust Forrest in anything much more than partisan campaigns: they seemed unable to believe a non-West Pointer was up to major action.

Forrest began training his second group of greenhorns, and in the first raid of his new command led 1000 cavalrymen into Murfreesboro, Tennessee, in July, to surprise a Federal encampment. Ordered to slow the advance of the main Union army toward the rail center of Chattanooga and to support Bragg's invasion of Kentucky, he did both in spades over the next months. His riders captured Murfreesboro entire, with its over 1000 Federals and supplies worth upward of a million dollars. They then rode out to rout a garrison at Lebanon, wreak havoc on Federal rail lines, and brush away the Federals sent to chase them. By the end of July Federal operations in Tennessee and Kentucky were threatened and Forrest was a brigadier general. (Bragg soon aborted his Kentucky invasion, typically, just as it was showing promise.)

Raiding west Tennessee in December, Forrest cut Grant's rail supply line, whipped Federal cavalry at Lexington, and uprooted rails for miles into Kentucky. At the end of the year he was finally stymied by Federals who caught his force between two columns at Parker's Crossroads. Legend recounts that when his officers pointed out this problem and asked what to do about it, Forrest replied, 'Charge them both ways.' In any case, that is what his men did, setting the enemy back on their heels long enough for the Confederates to squeeze out. They left behind, however, their nine guns and most of their captured property. Nothing daunted, in March 1863 Forrest captured 1500 Federals and their supplies at Thompson's Station and two weeks later over-ran a fortified camp at Brentwood, where his haul included 35 commissioned officers.

Likewise undaunted, Grant prepared to launch his campaign to take Vicksburg, which would end Southern control of the Mississippi. Having had quite enough from Forrest and his men, the Federals decided to run these Rebels aground to keep them from troubling Grant or Rosecrans's new Union offensive on Chattanooga.

In April 1863 Rosecrans dispatched Colonel Abel D Streight into Alabama with mule-mounted troops to raid and to chase Forrest down. Instead, Streight found himself closely pursued, Forrest worrying his column day and night. For two weeks the Federals struggled on in growing exhaustion, the Rebels matching them mile for mile with apparent impunity. Actually, the Confederates were themselves near collapse when a young girl showed them a shortcut that allowed Forrest to get in front of Streight, who finally asked for a truce. As they conferred, Forrest kept his two cannon circling around – a common trick with him – until the Union commander exclaimed, 'Name of God! How many guns have you got? There's fifteen I've counted already.' Forrest blandly replied, 'I reckon that's all that has kept up.' Soon the Confederate troops were at the same game, and Streight caved in to apparently overwhelming odds. He was chagrined to discover he had surrendered his 1466 men to Forrest's 500.

Not long after this Forrest was wounded again, this time by his own subordinate, A Wills Gould, who was enraged at a transfer Forrest had forced upon him. During an argument Gould shot his commander point-blank in the side. Forrest grabbed his assailant's pistol hand, opened a pen-knife with his teeth, and stabbed Gould in the stomach. There followed a chase through the streets of Columbia, Tennessee, the wounded and bellowing Forrest sprinting after the mortally wounded Gould. A few days later the two had a tearful reconciliation as Gould lay dying and Forrest himself not too far from it.

That was in June 1863. By September Forrest was well and serving under Braxton Bragg when the latter met Rosecrans at Chickamauga, just past Chattanooga into Georgia. The Confederacy, having lost Vicksburg to Grant and seen Lee fail at Gettysburg, was starved for a victory. And Bragg's army provided one, breaking the Union line at Chickamauga on 19 September. But by failing to pursue the routed Federals, Bragg set in

Sketch depicting a typical Virginia Military Academy cadet.

Officially classed as a 'gun-howitzer,' the 12-pounder Napoleon took the brunt of the artillery's war. This model represented the zenith of the smoothbore.

motion the process that would lead to Grant's victory in Chattanooga and Sherman's march across Georgia.

Seeing Bragg's failure, and moreover severed from his command without explanation, an apoplectic Forrest accosted Bragg and raged in high form: 'You robbed me of my command in Kentucky. You drove me into West Tennessee in the winter of 1862 with a second brigade I had organized, with improper arms and without sufficient ammunition ... and now this second brigade ... you have taken from me. I have stood your meanness as long as I intend to. You have played the part of a damned scoundrel, and if you were any part of a man I would slap your jaws and force you to resent it. You may as well not issue any orders to me, for I will not obey them. If you ever again try to interfere with me or cross my path it will be at the peril of your life.'

With that he stormed off to Richmond to resign; Bragg meanwhile took no punitive action, perhaps suspecting Forrest was right. Being a poor judge of generals but not an utter fool, Jefferson Davis gave Forrest an independent command and sent him off raiding in west Tennessee again, and to boot made him a major general.

It was then that Forrest commenced the primary task of his military career: being a full-time nemesis to Federal General William Tecumseh Sherman. By the beginning of 1864 Grant had chased Bragg from Chattanooga and Sherman's army was preparing for its historic campaign in Georgia. Concerned for his vulnerable supply line, Sherman ordered General W Sooy Smith to neutralize Forrest. That proved to be much more easily ordered than done; on 21 February Forrest scattered Smith's column of 7000 cavalry. Next day the Federals attempted a stand at Okolona, and for their temerity were chased 60 miles back to Memphis, less five cannon and many men.

Having humbled Smith, Forrest turned to a Union garrison called Fort Pillow, on the Mississippi River near Jackson, Tennessee. The fort was manned by under 600 Federals, half of them, as it happened, black troops. (The Union had formed black regiments and was finding them adept and enthusiastic soldiers.) Moreover, the white troops in the fort were largely men from Tennessee, whom Confederates scornfully referred to as 'renegades' or 'homemade Yankees.'

Fort Pillow was ripe for the picking, and Forrest sent General James R Chalmers with 1500 cavalrymen to pick it. On 12 April 1864 Chalmers arrived at dawn, drove in the pickets, and invested the fort. Arriving about 10:00 in the morning, Forrest looked things over and saw that he could get his men in positions from which they could assault without being reachable either by the garrison's guns or those of a Federal gunboat on the river.

His men in place by mid-afternoon, Forrest sent in his usual ultimatum: surrender or no quarter. The acting Federal commander, Major William F Bradford, asked for and was granted an

Jefferson Davis, president of the Confederacy.

US Cavalry troops prepare for battle.

hour's truce to think it over. At that point confusion set in, which in its train brought a horror that was to reverberate through North and South, and history as well.

During the truce each side made movements the other side took as threatening, and Forrest soon called for an immediate answer. It came – a refusal. Forrest ordered the bugle to sound the charge, and his troopers bolted out, leaping ditches and parapets while Rebel sharpshooters plinked away at any Yankee head appearing over the fort. The Confederate riders clattered down into a 12-foot ditch, splashed through the mud at the bottom and up the other side – not a shot yet fired – then dismounted and helped one another up the walls. There followed a brief and intense

The 107th US Colored Infantry. Blacks enlisted in and were recruited by the Union army beginning in 1863; by the end of the war they numbered about 300,000.

A Confederate sharpshooter.

exchange of point-blank fire with pistol and rifle; before the Federals could reload, the second wave of attackers was over and emptying their guns into the close ranks of the Yankees.

With most of their officers fallen, the defenders broke and ran. Confusion multiplied. Apparently there was no official Federal surrender, perhaps no one left having the authority to surrender. As individuals and as groups, some Federals threw down their arms and gave up, others ran for the gunboat on the river with Rebels at their heels, others picked up guns and resumed fighting after surrendering. Then the horror began. Before Forrest arrived on the scene, unarmed Federals were being massacred.

The exact facts of what happened remain obscure. It was later to be to the North's advantage to picture as monstrous an atrocity as possible, to the South's advantage to deny everything. Certainly Forrest had not ordered a massacre of surrendered men, and he stopped the killing when he arrived. Just as certainly, some killing in cold blood had already occurred. It is likely that some Southerners were heard crying, 'No quarter! Kill the damned niggers! Shoot them down!' As for the other stories – men nailed to trees and set aflame, black men buried alive, and the rest – history has never decided. The casualty figures say much: 127 whites died, 204 blacks, together more than half the Federals killed. Confederate losses were 14 killed, 86 wounded. Forrest wrote in a letter, 'The river was dyed with the blood of the slaughtered for two hundred yards. ... It is hoped that these facts will demonstrate to the Northern people that Negro soldiers cannot cope with Southerners.'

Just over three weeks later Sherman pulled his army out of Chattanooga and headed for Atlanta. After taking Fort Pillow, Forrest spent some time resting and recruiting. Sherman, his supply line ever more vulnerable as he pushed south, sent another force to challenge Forrest: 3000 cavalry, 4800 infantry, and 18 guns, sent from Memphis under General S D Sturgis. Forrest, now with

4713 cavalry and eight cannon – about half his enemy's strength – determined to attack the on-coming Federals.

Forrest's orders of 10 June 1864 show both that he foresaw the exhaustion of the fast-marching Union infantry and also assumed his men would be ready and able to fight in the scorching weather: 'Their cavalry will move out ahead of their infantry and should reach [Brice's Cross Roads] three hours in advance. We can whip their cavalry in that time. As soon as the fight opens they will send back to have the infantry hurried up. It is going to be hot as hell, and coming on a run for five or six miles, their infantry will be so tired out we will ride right over them.'

It proved exactly as Forrest prophesied. At 9:30 in the morning Benjamin Grierson's Federal cavalry ran into Forrest's advance at Brice's Cross Roads, an insignificant crossing sporting three buildings. Skirmishing broke out between Grierson's 3200 men and the 900 Confederates on the scene. The Federals halted, and Grierson sent riders to reconnoiter. They soon ran into some Southern pickets, and Grierson realized he had a battle on his hands.

Few as they were, the Rebels mounted three charges at the enemy. These bluffs worked handsomely. The Yankees dismounted and began picking away at the Rebels, who fell back into the thick woods. As Forrest had also foreseen, these woods kept the bluecoats from seeing just how thin the Southern line was. Grierson made no move to test the enemy line but rather sent back to Sturgis asking that the Union infantry be hurried forward.

Moments of leisure in a military camp.

At one o'clock in the afternoon Grierson was still sitting, later reporting the enemy to be in place 'in large numbers, with double lines of skirmishers and line of battle, with heavy supports.' Once again Forrest's men had proven able actors. By then Forrest had most of his men and all his artillery moved up to the crossroads. Though still heavily outnumbered, Forrest launched the attack, soon pushing Grierson's line back on both flanks.

Each of the Confederates seemed to work like two men, fighting it out with bullets and clubbed carbines while the Southern artillery tore into the Union line. Arriving shortly after one o'clock with the first contingent of infantry, a Northern officer found the situation 'going to the devil as fast as it possibly could,' the Union line bent into a semicircle.

Having hurried up at double time in the searing heat, the Union infantry arrived utterly spent, dozens falling out with sunstroke, the officers convinced they were outnumbered. Now Forrest began to fight in earnest, giving the enemy no rest. Fixing the Federal line in place with steady pressure, he sent John Bell's cavalry brigade on a wide sweep around the Union left to the rear. As Bell's men fought their way through the dense underbrush, a lull came into the battle, men on both sides falling exhausted on their rifles. But Forrest had no intention of letting up. Riding along his line on a big sorrel, he roared, 'Get up,

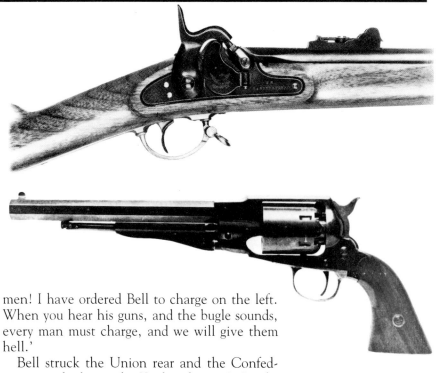

men! I have ordered Bell to charge on the left. When you hear his guns, and the bugle sounds, every man must charge, and we will give them hell.'

Bell struck the Union rear and the Confederates pitched into the Yankee front. A Southerner remembered of the charge, 'Guns once fired were used as clubs, and pistols were brought into play, while the two lines struggled with the ferocity of wild beasts.' As the opposing forces flailed away in the center, Bell's 250 men pressed hard onto the rear of the Federal left flank, widely deployed to exaggerate their strength. Meanwhile, another small contingent of Southerners

Top: Rifle with Maynard tape primer.

Above: The Remington 'New Model' Army, 1863.

Below: Samuel J Reader's *Double-quick, you Yankee!!!*

The Colt .36 calibre Navy Model 1851 was a popular sidearm of the Civil War.

began creeping around the enemy right flank.

Union General Sturgis, moving up his last reinforcements about five o'clock, found his flanks were crumpling. Soon a panic began, fleeing Federals pouring in dozens and then hundreds to the rear; the battle line disintegrated, the roads becoming, as a Union man recalled, 'one indiscriminate mass of wagons, artillery, caissons, ambulances, and broken, disordered troops,' all of them harried by Confederate artillerymen wielding not only their own but recently captured Federal cannons. Attempting to pursue, Forrest reported, 'The road was so blockaded with abandoned vehicles of every description that it was difficult to move the artillery forward.'

Picking their way through the debris, the Confederates pursued Sturgis until dark and took up the chase again at one o'clock in the morning. After 50 miles of skedaddling, the thoroughly demoralized Federals limped back into Memphis. Of his 7800 men Sturgis had lost 223 killed, 394 wounded, and 1623 captured, plus 16 of his 18 guns and 250 wagons. Forrest reported 492 casualties of 3500 engaged. The Battle of Brice's Cross Roads was Forrest's finest day. Soon Sherman would be howling, 'That devil Forrest must be hunted down and killed if it costs ten thousand lives and bankrupts the Federal treasury!'

Sherman did not expend 10,000 men, bankrupt any treasury, or ever catch Forrest. And for all his fury, in the end Sherman did not need to hunt down his devil: Sherman took Atlanta all the same, and in November of 1864 set out across Georgia with no supply line at all, burning and plundering his way to the sea. Forrest kept up his operations to the rear of Sherman's marauding army, always a threat, never quite a spoiler. In August Forrest and 1500 men raided the Federal garrison in Memphis, capturing guns and prisoners and causing panic among the Federals. At the end of September he took a 600-man Federal garrison at Athens, Alabama, and two weeks later crossed the Tennessee River, having captured 1200 men and 800 horses.

But by then it was all aftershocks, heroics for a cause already lost. In the last weeks of the war Forrest was given the exalted and empty rank of lieutenant general. He was powerless before the Union juggernaut as it moved into Alabama; that was his only real loss of the war. On 9 May 1865, just under a month after Lee's surrender at Appomattox, Forrest ordered his men to lay down their arms.

His later career lacked either the success or the glamor of his war years. He went into soldiering a millionaire and came out a pauper; his efforts to rebuild his fortune in planting and railroading failed. For several years he was Grand Wizard of the Ku Klux Klan, resigning his connection in 1869. He died in Memphis in 1877 at the age of 56.

Forrest had been a leader, as one of his officers later observed, 'greater than his opportunities.' His exploits, though none of them turned any tides of the South, had influence far out of proportion to the small number of troops he commanded. Among the myriad *ifs* of the war there will always remain the question: What if Forrest had been given a major command in the South? When General Joseph E Johnston, Sherman's adversary in the Atlanta campaign, was asked in later years whom he considered the greatest soldier of the war, without hestitation he named Nathan Bedford Forrest, 'who, had he had the advantages of a thorough military education . . . would have been the great central figure of the Civil War.'

A British military historian summed Forrest up in these words: 'Forrest had no knowledge of military history to teach him how he should act, what objective he should aim at, and what plans he should make to secure it. He was entirely ignorant of what other generals in previous wars had done under very similar circumstances. What he lacked in book-lore was to a large extent compensated for by the soundness of his judgment upon all great occasions, and by his power of thinking and reasoning with great rapidity under fire. Inspired with true military instincts, he was verily nature's soldier.'

Perhaps the most authentic testimony came from another general of the day, who called Forrest 'the most remarkable man the civil war produced on either side. . . . He had a genius for strategy which was original and to me incomprehensible.' That despairing admiration came from William Tecumseh Sherman, who had ample reason to know what he was talking about.

JOSEPH EGGLESTON JOHNSTON

Chattanooga to Atlanta

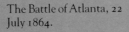

The Battle of Atlanta, 22 July 1864.

What makes a general 'great'? It cannot be because he won all the battles he was personally in command of: if that were the case, Robert E Lee would not be universally regarded as among the great generals of modern times. History does not accord greatness to a general on the basis of such quantifiable matters as victories or casualties. There is something less tangible, something about the way a general conducted himself in action, as well as the way he carried out his strategy and tactics, that gains him the reputation summed up by 'great.'

Never was this more apposite than in considering the Civil War career of Joseph Eggleston Johnston. For here is a man who was perceived by many of his peers – on both sides of the Civil War – as a great general and yet who can hardly be credited with any major victory, if that is defined as a battle where he controlled the strategy and/or the tactics and led his forces to unequivocal triumph over opposing forces. Not only can Johnston claim no such major victory, he spent much of his Civil War career withdrawing, if not

Jefferson Davis often disagreed with Joseph Johnston's strategy throughout the war.

actually retreating, form Federal forces. He was even removed from two major commands by his own superiors in the Confederate Government. What makes it all the more astonishing is that throughout the Civil War, while many of the Federal generals would continue to express their high regard for Johnston, he found himself carrying on a running battle with many of his fellow Confederate generals and, above all, with President Jefferson Davis.

From the moment Johnston accepted the rank of major general from the governor of Virginia, John Letcher, barely 48 hours after Robert E Lee had accepted a similar commission, until the final days of the Confederacy – indeed, to the final days of Johnston's life – his Civil War career was marked by controversy and conflict. It is almost heartbreaking to read of Johnston's continual disagreements and disputes in the correspondence and reports of the time, and although he may have had a slightly touchy side when it came to matters of rank and honor, he was far from being the most disputatious of the Civil War generals. Somehow, though, Joseph E Johnston found himself fighting a civil war on two fronts – against the Federals and against many Confederates, most especially their difficult and often quarrelsome President, Jefferson Davis.

After accepting the rank of major general in Virginia's forces, for instance, Johnston in mid-May went to Montgomery, Alabama, where Jefferson Davis then had his headquarters, and accepted the rank of brigadier general in the Army of the Confederacy, firmly expecting to be promoted to full general and, with that rank and seniority, placed in command of the Confederate forces in Virginia. Johnston's critics and detractors claim to this day that Johnston went to Montgomery primarily to advance his own career, and in particular, make sure Robert E Lee was not given the command first. His friends and supporters insist that his only reason for going to obtain his commission from President Davis was that he, Johnston, recognized that the Confederate armed forces must have a unified command, that an effective opposition could not be mounted if each state were to field its own army with its own chain of command. This would seem a relatively academic and irrelevant issue except that these very matters – rank, seniority, and chain of command – would bedevil Johnston throughout the Civil War, as to a lesser degree they would bedevil other Confederate generals.

In any case, Johnston was assigned by the Confederate Army to take command of the Army of the Shenandoah with his headquarters at Harper's Ferry, Virginia. Harper's Ferry is about 50 miles northwest of Washington, DC, and sits at the junction of the Potomac and Shenandoah Rivers and on the then crucial point where the Baltimore and Ohio Railroad crossed the Potomac. It was regarded by some within the Confederacy as also guarding the route from Pennsylvania into the Shenandoah Valley, a

route that Union forces would most certainly want to take. Johnston arrived at Harper's Ferry on 23 May 1861, and it was not long before he came to conclude that its strategic importance had been distorted; he decided, in fact, that the Union forces could easily overwhelm it, go around it, or just simply take another route from the North into Virginia. He began to convey these views to the Confederate authorities in Richmond, where Jefferson Davis had moved with the government on 29 May. Both Davis and Lee, however, asked him to plan to hold Harper's Ferry, in part because of the arsenal there and in part because of the symbolic and political repercussions should the Confederates forces pull out.

Johnston thus embarked on the first of what would be an almost continuous series of arguments – largely through military channels and usually couched in formally respectful language – with the authorities in Richmond and his fellow Confederate commanders, mainly over the broader strategy of the war and the tactics to be pursued in the field. In particular, Johnston found himself constantly disagreeing with Jefferson Davis. But that lay in the future when in mid-June Johnston took it upon himself to move his forces and headquarters from Harper's Ferry to Winchester, a town some 25 miles to the south and located at a point he regarded as more strategic. (The order from Richmond authorizing Johnston's evacuation of Harper's Ferry arrived over 24 hours after Johnston had begun to do just that.)

Johnston's withdrawal to Winchester and his refusal to move against the Federal forces that were beginning to threaten northern Virginia inevitably led to some criticism, although this was one of several instances when Jefferson Davis, at least in a letter, supported Johnston.

'The anxiety of the reckless and the short-sighted policy of the selfish may urge you to fight when your judgment decides otherwise,' wrote Davis. 'Follow the dictates of your own good judgment and true patriotism.' The soundness of Johnston's judgment became apparent in mid-July, when the Federal forces commanded by General Irvin McDowell began to move toward the Confederate army at Manassas Junction, a strategic railroad junction only about 30 miles from Washington, DC and 75 miles from Richmond. At Winchester Johnston was about 50 miles northwest of Manassas Junction, but he was in telegraph communication with Richmond – as was General P T G Beauregard, the Confederate commander at Manassas Junction – and he was thus in a position to move his troops to support those of Beauregard when Richmond gave the orders to do so on July 18. Had Johnston remained in Harper's Ferry, he might well have been held in check there by the Federal forces under General Robert Patterson, but now he was able to sneak the bulk of his 10,000-man force out of Winchester. Then, in what was the first use of the railroad for strategic mobility, Johnston

Major-General McClellan, Major-General McDowell and staffs, escorted by the Fifth Cavalry, cross Bull Run at Blackburn's Ford.

The Bridge over Bull Run, near Blackburn's Ford, burned by the rebels.

The Confederate naval
battery at Manassas
Junction, Virginia

Opposite: Major General Irvin McDowell (1818-1885) commanded the Federal forces at First Manassas, where his green troops could not withstand the Confederates.

Colonel Michael Corcoran leads the desperate charge of the 'Gallant Sixty Ninth' on the Rebel batteries at First Manassas.

moved his 10,000 men by the Manassas Gap Railroad for the last 35 miles or so.

Up to his arrival at Manassas Junction Johnston's role in the imminent battle was essentially one of reacting to others' plans, including his decision to ignore some of General Beauregard's more risky plans. Now on the scene, however, he was careful to discuss all the possible options with Beauregard and to arrive at an agreement: they would take the offensive against McDowell's forces before they could be reinforced by Patterson's troops. However, the Federals moved on the offensive early on the morning of 21 July and forced the Confederates to react. But the Confederates made the right moves, realizing which were the secondary feints and which was the main attack – a wide enveloping by McDowell's right wing – and responding appropriately. Because Beauregard was more familiar with the area, he directed the operations on the line while Johnston oversaw the overall flow of the Confederate forces, sending up reinforcements where needed, assigning the last-minute arrivals (by rail and overland) of his troops from Winchester. At first the Federal flanking move forced the Confederates to pull back to Henry House Hill, but a brigade led by Brigadier General Thomas Jackson stood firm and the advancing Federals were stopped. With the arrival of reinforcements, Jackson was able to mount a counterattack during the afternoon, and by four o'clock the Federals were in full retreat. They crossed back over the Bull Run Creek – which the Union side would adopt as their name for the battle – and by the

next day the disorganized remnants of McDowell's army made their way into Washington, DC. The Federals had suffered about 3000 casualties (dead, wounded, or missing) to the Confederates' 2000, and the Battle of Manassas, or Bull Run, at once became the victory that the Confederacy needed to inspire its struggle.

For General Johnston it was not a total triumph. At a meeting that evening with General Beauregard and President Davis – who, as he would do so often during the war, had ridden out to the scene of the battle – there was some confusion as to whether a full-scale pursuit of the Federals should be mounted the next morning. Johnston would always insist that no such order was given by Davis, and so the Confederates allowed the retreating Federals to make their way back to Washington unmolested. Johnston, Davis, and Beauregard would spend the rest of their lives disagreeing about who was responsible for this failure to follow through after the First Battle of Manassas, but it would be used by Johnston's detractors as one more example of his failure to take the offensive. Meanwhile, in the immediate aftermath of the battle, General Beauregard, already a Southern hero because he had commanded the attack on Fort Sumter, got most of the popular credit, although the Confederate Senate did pass a resolution of appreciation for both Johnston and Beauregard. Then, soon after, when Davis began to be criticized for not ordering the Confederate forces at Manassas to pursue the Federals all the way to Washington – and, or so it was presumed, forcing the Federal

Pierre Gustave Toutant Beauregard became the Confederacy's first hero at Fort Sumter, and as a commander of the line at the First Bull Run he also gained the Confederacy its first victory on the battlefield.

capital to sue for peace – he requested Johnston to issue a public statement relieving him of the charge that he had 'obstructed the pursuit of the enemy.' Johnston did so immediately, but in so doing shifted the blame to himself.

In the months that followed the Confederate victory at Manassas Johnston found himself stymied by some of the same distracting and demeaning disputes that would continually plague the Confederate leadership. He became engaged in a rather bitter argument with Davis over whether he should be the senior ranking general of the Confederate army; he had problems with the reorganization of the Confederate army; as winter approached, he had troubles getting sufficient food and supplies for his troops; and above all, he carried on a running battle with the Confederate Secretary of War, Judah P Benjamin, over the latter's interference in matters that Johnston felt were the prerogative of the generals. The upshot of all this was that when March 1862 came around, the Confederate troops under Johnston in northern Virginia had not only engaged in little combat since Manassas, but they were now to be pulled back across the Rappahannock to be in a better position to defend Richmond from threatened Federal attacks from the east or south. Some units were left at Fredericksburg and elsewhere along the Rappahannock, others were moved still closer to Richmond, to the Rapidan River line. Once again it was Johnston who took responsibility for this withdrawal, and although Davis seemed to agree with the necessity and soundness of such a deployment of troops, he would in later years attempt to blame this 'hasty retreat' on Johnston. In fact, Johnston had one consistent strategy from the outset to the end of his command in Virginia: to keep Richmond from falling into the

hands of the Union. Lee, too, held to that strategy, and although Lee undeniably took a more aggressive route to that goal, it can be argued that it was only because of Johnston's prior decisions that Lee had the forces available to continue the fight.

No sooner had Johnston moved his forces to the Rappahannock and Rapidan lines than he had to deal with a new threat. On 24 March the Confederate leadership in Richmond received word that the Union was moving large numbers of men and weapons onto the tip of the peninsula formed by the James and York Rivers. The Federals were landing at Old Point Comfort near Fort Monroe, a strongly fortified US Army fort that would remain a thorn in the flank of the Confederacy throughout the entire war. (Ironically, it had been Robert E Lee who, as a young army engineer, had strengthened Fort Monroe and made it impregnable.) Confederate forces in this part of Virginia were concentrated at Yorktown and at Norfolk, but they were clearly no match for the growing Federal army, not to mention the Federals' powerful artillery, and once again it fell to Johnston to order a withdrawal. He came to this decision by 14 April, after visiting the Confederate positions in the Peninsula, but after a meeting with Davis, Lee, the Secretary of War, and other Confederate military leaders, he was overruled and told to

Right: Judah Philip Benjamin, the Confederate Secretary of War, disagreed with Johnston over military matters, and in March 1862 was transferred by Davis to be Secretary of State.

prepare to defend the Peninsula.

Though convinced that the Confederate forces there would be no match for the growing Federal forces, Johnston immediately took up his new command post at Yorktown and set about strengthening all possible defenses. By 3 May he felt sure that his troops were close to being trapped, and he began the withdrawal up the Peninsula. On 5 May his rear guard fought a fairly costly battle outside Williamsburg: the Confederates had some 1600 casualties, but the Federals had at least 2200. The commander of the Federal forces moving up the Peninsula, General George B McClellan, claimed it as a Union victory, but Johnston regarded it as an action that allowed him both to continue his withdrawal and to signal that the Confederates had plenty of fight in them. By 9 May Norfolk also had to be abandoned, a costly loss of a naval yard that the Confederacy would never be able to replace; moreover, it forced the Confederates to destroy their ironclad, the *Virginia* – as the Confederates had rechristened the *Merrimac*. On 15 May a Federal flotilla that was trying to approach Richmond by the James River was turned back by artillery from Drewry's Bluff. By 17 May Johnston had gathered the main elements of the Army of Northern Virginia in an arc only a few miles outside Richmond to protect the capital from attacks from the north, east, and south. He was now in a position to test the soundness of his long-held strategy.

Facing Johnston's army of some 42,000 men from just across the Chickahominy River was the Federal army of at least 100,000, commanded by General McClellan. But there were other Federal armies threatening smaller Confederate forces elsewhere in northern Virginia, and although Johnston was by no means in command of all the day-to-day events, it was his basic strategy that

Above: Battery No. 4 near Yorktown mounting ten 13-inch mortars.

Below: Union General Philip Kearney leads his troops at Williamsburg.

Major General George
Brinton McClellan (1826-
1885) faced Johnston, then
Lee, at Seven Pines.

Captain Porter's
Massachusetts Battery shells
Confederate forces across
the swollen Chickahominy.

was now being adhered to by the Confederates.
The first true test of Johnston's plan came on 31
May, when he launched an attack against some
42,000 Federals who had crossed to the south of
the Chickahominy and were digging in at Seven
Pines, about nine miles east of Richmond. Johnston had called for the attack to commence at
dawn, but through a series of misunderstandings,
poor communications, and just plain snafus, it

was not until about one in the afternoon that the
Confederates began their attack. Even then it
began with far fewer troops than Johnston had
called for, despite which the Confederates, by
taking severe casualties, were able to defeat the
Federals at the center of the line. This left some
Federal troops cut off at Fair Oaks, a point where
a main road crossed the Richmond-York River
Railroad, and Johnston himself directed the
attack against these forces late that afternoon.

As the battle dragged on into the evening,
Johnston ordered his men to plan to spend the
night at their posts and then resume fighting the
next morning. He had barely given this order
when he was struck by a musketball in his right
shoulder, then knocked unconscious from his
horse when a shell fragment struck his chest.
When he regained consciousness, he found himself being comforted by none other than Jefferson
Davis, who had as usual ridden out to the battle.
And then, in an episode so typical of Joseph
Eggleston Johnston, he realized he was missing
his sword and pistols (removed by his staff after he
fell from his horse). 'That sword was the one worn
by my father in the Revolutionary war and I
would not lose it for $10,000!' he exclaimed.
'Will not someone please go back and get it and
the pistols for me.' One of his couriers braved
heavy enemy fire to do just that, and Johnston
acknowledged his action by presenting him with
one of the pistols. In that little episode, with its

suggestion of tradition, dedication, and gallantry focused on a symbol, lies perhaps the key to what qualifies Johnston as a 'great' general.

Johnston was taken by horse-drawn ambulance to Richmond, and the next day Robert E Lee took over command of the Army of Northern Virginia. Lee surveyed the situation along the Fair Oaks-Seven Pines line and decided that the Confederates had lost the momentum. He ordered them to fall back to their previous positions. They had taken some 6100 casualties to the Federals' 5000, but Johnston's essential strategy had been vindicated: the Federals were not going to be able to take Richmond without a terrible struggle. This was borne out in the so-called Seven Days' Battles that Lee fought in the final week of June, effectively drawing upon the Confederate forces that Johnston had brought up to Richmond and now using them to drive the Federals all the way back down the Peninsula and removing the immediate threat to Richmond. Johnston was the first to recognize that Lee had succeeded in a way that he might not have been able to do, and also that Lee had the full support of President Davis and his advisers as he could never expect to have it.

Indeed, the career and reputation of Joseph Eggleston Johnston in the Civil War often seemed a mirror image of Lee's. Both men were much alike in many ways, their lives closely intertwined. Yet as Johnston's reputation fell ever closer to the nadir, Lee's seemed constantly to rise to the zenith. The father of Johnston who had carried that sword in the Revolution had fought under 'Light Horse Harry' Lee – Robert E Lee's father. Johnston, like Lee, was a true son of Virginia; they had known each other as youths, then entered West Point in the same class. They became close friends there and in the years following graduation their military assignments often brought them together. They shared a cabin on the ship taking the US Army to Veracruz in 1847 and fought together in the expedition that ended with the taking of Mexico City. In the ensuing years the two officers drew different assignments, but both rose in rank and reputation. In June 1860, in fact, Johnston was appointed Quartermaster General of the US Army, a post that Lee rather hoped to get. In the end, Johnston did not get to hold that post very long, for by April 1861 he followed Lee in resigning from the US Army, and for the same reason: as Johnston told the governor of Virginia, my 'sword would never be drawn against [my] native state.' But the factor that always seemed to make the difference between Lee's and Johnston's reputations throughout the Civil War was the very one that Johnston recognized after Lee took over his command that June of 1862: 'Then, my wound was fortunate. . . . Lee had made them do for him what they would not do for me.'

'What they would not do for me' refers to Johnston's continual complaint that the Confederate Government in Richmond, in particu-

Above: A posed photograph of General George Stoneman and staff at Fair Oaks, Virginia, in June 1862.

lar, Jefferson Davis, would seldom support his strategy and his calls for troops. Never was this to be more agonizingly the case than in the months that followed Johnston's return to active duty in November 1862. He had spent the summer recovering from his wounds, but by 13 November he was given a new assignment: command of the 'Division of the West,' a sort of 'super headquarters' that was to supervise the departments commanded by Braxton Bragg, John Pemberton, and F Kirby Smith. On the surface it seemed a major honor and responsibility for Johnston, especially since Jefferson Davis's dislike of him was hardly a secret. In practice it turned out to be a position of utter frustration. To begin with, it was a somewhat ill-defined geographical command lying between the Blue Ridge Mountains and the Mississippi River, and the Confederate army was not organized under such boundaries. Furthermore, it was such a large area that Johnston would often be unable to maintain communications with the commanders in the field. But the most demeaning, and dooming, aspect of the assignment was that the chain of command was not clearly defined, so that the various department commanders did not report directly to Johnston but were usually getting their orders from Richmond. 'Nobody ever assumed a command under more unfavorable circumstances,' Johnston wrote to a friend at the outset, and there as so often he proved to be most prescient.

Johnston arrived in Chattanooga on 4 December 1862 to take up his command, and almost immediately became embroiled in a quarrel with Davis over the disposition of troops along the Mississippi. Johnston immediately recognized that the river port of Vicksburg was of utmost strategic importance to the Confederacy, and he tried to get Davis to authorize the transfer of more

Above: A Louisiana 'Pelican.'

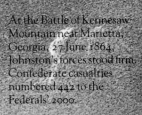

At the Battle of Kennesaw
Mountain near Marietta,
Georgia, 27 June 1864,
Johnston's forces stood firm.
Confederate casualties
numbered 442 to the
Federals' 2000.

'Teazer' gun on a
Confederate gunboat.

troops to the Vicksburg area. Davis would never authorize this, and by April 1863 Grant had clearly committed his forces to taking Vicksburg. Here again Johnston differed from the commander in the field, General John Pemberton, who, against Johnston's advice, withdrew his forces into Vicksburg, where they soon become immobilized by the great siege that led to the surrender of Vicksburg on 4 July. By 16 July Johnston was forced to abandon Jackson, Mississippi. These losses, along with the defeat at Gettysburg, left the Confederacy feeling despondent, even devastated, and Johnston inevitably came in for a great deal of criticism. In fact, he spent much of his energy in the following months simply defending himself against the charges from Davis and his supporters, both in the military and civilian sectors of the Confederacy, that he was responsible for the loss of Vicksburg.

Then came the battle at Chickamauga (19-20 September) and the climax of the Federal attack at Chattanooga (23-5 November), with the result that General Braxton Bragg was thoroughly discredited and forced to resign his command over the Army of Tennessee. Many of those best informed about the situation in the Western Theater knew of Johnston's true role and now encouraged Davis to appoint him to succeed Bragg. On 16 December Johnston received this command from Davis, but any hope that this signified a change in Davis's inimical attitude toward him would soon be disappointed.

Johnston took over command of a dispirited army of about 42,000 men when he set up his headquarters in Dalton, Georgia, a small rail center about 25 miles southeast of Chattanooga.

It had been a year of set-backs for the Confederate cause. On 31 December 1863, the Richmond (Virginia) *Examiner* observed that 'Today closes the gloomiest year of our struggle.' Nevertheless, Johnson set about trying to build up his army, in numbers, discipline and equipment. By the spring of 1864 Johnston had about 62,000 men in his army, but he would never have enough men and materiel to hold off the powerful Federal army commanded by General William T Sherman. It was with this army of some 100,000 that Sherman moved down into Georgia on 7 May to begin his campaign to take Atlanta, and it was from this army that Johnston found himself forced to retreat week after week. There were actions and engagements – at Rocky Face Ridge (5-9 May), at Resaca (13-16 May), at Cassville (19 May), at Dallas, or New Hope Church (25-7 May) – when Johnston held Sherman off valiantly, but each time felt compelled to the painful decision that he could not risk his men in an all-out stand. Finally, Johnston made a stand at Kennesaw Mountain, where Sherman mounted a full-scale attack on 27 June; by the 29th, the Confederates had held their own, and suffered only about one-seventh as many casualties as the Federals. Recognizing, nevertheless, that it was only a matter of time before Sherman could bring up far more troops, Johnston pulled back to the Chattahoochee River, only some 10 miles northwest of the city limits of Atlanta. By now Johnston had taken some 9000 casualties and he was becoming desperate for reinforcements, but Davis seemed unable to come up with any. There were increasing calls from Richmond for more aggressive action, ignoring what Johnston knew too sadly well that such action could, probably would, mean the annihilation of his troops. On 9 July he withdrew once again, this time a few miles south of the Chattahoochee to Peach Tree Creek. Jefferson Davis, meanwhile, was only too pre-disposed to listen to those among his military and civilian advisers who were anxious to blame Johnston for the defeats of the Confederacy, and on 17 July he removed Johnston from command and replaced him by General John B Hood. It was the second time within a little over two years that Johnston was removed from a major command.

Once again he was plunged into a public and private debate over the wisdom of his strategy and the courage (or cowardice?) of his tactics. Those who were against Johnston pointed to the fact that Hood did take the offensive, but con-veniently forgot that Hood inevitably had to surrender Atlanta anyway. As the debate raged among all levels of Confederate society, Johnston at first settled in Atlanta, then was forced to move on to Macon, Georgia, and then to Columbia, South Carolina. When Sherman began his campaign north from Savannah in February 1865, pressure was put on Davis to re-store Johnston to command, and on 23 February Johnston did take back command of the Army of Tennessee, along with all other troops available in South Carolina, Georgia, and Florida.

But to all except the most diehard Confed-erates, the end was clearly in sight, and Johnston could at best fight some delaying battles. This he did, maintaining discipline and pride in his re-treating army and even inflicting heavy losses on the Federals in such battles as that at Bentonville, North Carolina (19 March). With the surrender by Lee at Appomattox Court House on 9 April, possibly only Jefferson Davis believed that the Confederacy was not at an end. At a meeting on 13 April with his cabinet, to which General Johnston had been summoned, Davis was still claiming, 'I think we can whip the enemy yet, if our people will turn out.' Johnston then spoke out, stating bluntly that since the Confederacy was 'without money, or credit, or arms, or ammunition, or means of procuring them,' con-tinuing the war 'would be the greatest of human crimes.' Davis reluctantly authorized Johnston to try to arrange an armistice with Sherman, and on 26 April Johnston surrendered his army, thus effectively ending the Civil War, although spor-adic skirmishes continued west of the Mississippi.

Johnston's days as a general were over. In the years following the war he worked with insurance and railroad companies, and served a term in Congress. He also found himself engaged in the ongoing 'war of words' that forced him to defend his strategy and actions in the Civil War. But leaders on both sides of the sad conflict – Robert E Lee, William Tecumseh Sherman, Ulysses S Grant – who had fought with or against him and who themselves truly understood the obligations of command, never lost their respect for John-ston. They of all men knew that it was his loyalty, his compassion, his judgment, that had made Joseph Eggleston Johnston one of the great generals of the Civil War.

James Bennett's house, where Johnston surrendered to Sherman.

WILLIAM TECUMSEH SHERMAN

Siege of Atlanta
March to the Sea

General Sherman arrives at
Savannah, Georgia.

In the last year of the war, April 1864 to April 1865, only two principal Confederate armies remained: the Army of Northern Virginia, led by Robert E Lee, about 60,000 strong, protecting the Confederate capital of Richmond; and the Army of Tennessee, about the same size, commanded by Joseph Eggleston Johnston, strongly entrenched in northern Georgia. The Confederacy also had considerable forces west of the Mississippi, but Federal control of the river since Vicksburg relegated events in the trans-Mississippi region to a position of minor importance.

U S Grant, now in command of all Federal armies and giving the Union its first co-ordinated plan of action since the beginning of the war, correctly saw that the fate of the Confederacy rested upon the fate of Lee's and Johnston's armies. He wanted these armies destroyed as quickly as possible. As far as he was concerned, the capture of cities and strategic points and the occupation of Southern territory meant very little. As he prepared to move against Lee's army and General Benjamin F Butler readied his Army of the James to move against Richmond, Grant ordered Major General William Tecumseh Sherman, now in command of the whole Western theater with the exception of the Banks expedition, to move against Johnston.

With habitual energy and imagination, Sherman had been gathering supplies since December for a new offensive into the heart of the Confederacy. To ensure the safety of his communications, he created a movable railroad repair base with trained crews, which proved so successful that Confederate soldiers were to create the legend that his Yankee troops carried duplicate tunnels and bridges with them. Knowing he could not be bound entirely to the railroad, he organized a system of horse-and-wagon transportation that would provide adequate supplies when he left the Atlantic and Western Railroad; and he studied United States census reports and tax rolls of Georgia's counties in order to predict prime forage areas for his men and animals. The coming campaign would also see Sherman's introduction of map coordinates, photographic duplication of maps, trip wires, and a looser and more extended order of infantry attack. By the time he moved out after Johnston toward Atlanta in the campaign that was to turn into the March to the Sea, he had, among other innovations, transformed engineering into a major factor in modern warfare.

Three years earlier, on 14 May 1861, Sherman had accepted command as colonel of the 13th Infantry in the hastily expanded US Army, having previously spurned the offer of a commission as a major general of volunteers. As a West Point man, he had no wish to be associated with citizen soldiers; he had already declined the offer of a high commission in the Confederate Army, despite a deep and genuine affection for the South, where he had lived for about 12 years. The last two, as superintendent of a new military college in Louisiana (now Louisiana State University), had been the happiest and most successful in a civilian career marked by failure as a lawyer and a banker following his resignation from the army in 1853. But regardless of his love for the South, when Louisiana seceded, he chose the Union. He was anguished by the prospect of civil war, but believed in the preservation of the Union with a fundamental, almost religious, fervor. If war had to come, he felt it ought to be brought to a conclusion as swiftly as possible.

In his first battle experience Sherman commanded a brigade of green troops at the First Battle of Bull Run, or Manassas, the first major land engagement of the war. A confused action which ended in a panic and rout of the Union troops, it convinced him that he was unfit for the responsibility of an independent command. He

General Robert Anderson, whom Sherman served under in Kentucky until Anderson fell ill; Sherman was then appointed commander of the Department of the Cumberland.

asked to be spared further such responsibility, but Lincoln promoted him to brigadier general of volunteers and sent him to serve as second-in-command in Kentucky under General Robert Anderson. He had apparently extracted an agreement from someone in Washington to the effect that he would never be asked to take command, but Anderson's health failed, and Sherman inherited the thankless task of trying to hold the Department of the Cumberland with little more than home guards.

Nervous, high-strung, and overwhelmed, he panicked. He was well aware that Washington had woefully underestimated the South's seriousness of intent (Lincoln had originally asked for 75,000 volunteers for three months to put down the rebellion), and saw on every hand increasing dangers from increasing numbers of Confederate

Top: General Burnside's brigade at the Battle of Bull Run.
Above: Sherman and his generals. Left to right: O O Howard, Hugh Judson Kilpatrick, John A Logan, General Hazen, Sherman, Jefferson Davis, Henry Slocum, Francis P Blair and J A Mower.

General William Tecumseh Sherman (1820-1891) came to be regarded as one of the North's most successful military heroes, but the South would always consider him as the archenemy because of his infamous march to Atlanta and the sea.

troops. His demands on Washington for heavier and heavier reinforcements prompted Secretary of War Simon Cameron to visit him in Louisville. The party accompanying Cameron included several newspaper reporters; and Sherman, red-haired and red-bearded with the temperament to match, pacing the room excitedly and gesticulating and talking in his customary volcanic manner, made a bad impression. His demands for 60,000 men for defensive purposes and 200,000 men for offense would not seem too extreme in retrospect, but at the time they were extraordinary, and at any rate impossible for the government to raise. Taken with his emotional presentation, his demands led the press to imply that he was insane. Regardless of later developments, his demands were in fact less the estimate of a cool and analytical mind than of a fevered and distraught imagination. He later told his brother Senator John Sherman that he had disgraced himself by exaggerating the enemy's forces in Kentucky, did not think he could again be entrusted with a command, and had been prevented from suicide only by his duty to his children.

It has been said that no American soldier ever disliked reporters more than Sherman did. Regardless of his previous feelings, the treatment he received from the press in Kentucky permanently embittered him. Throughout the war he considered all reporters liars at best and Confederate agents at worst. At Vicksburg, long after he had more than redeemed himself as a commander, he was undoubtedly responsible for much of the bad press the campaign got in the North, as well as for the newspaper attacks against Grant, whose approach to the inevitable innovation of constant battlefront press coverage was sanguine and manipulative. Sherman, ranting that he was 'a spy and an infamous dog,' in fact had reporter Tom Knox of the *New York Herald* court-martialed at Vicksburg, largely because Knox had had the misfortune to misunderstand Sherman's hyperbolic manner, and recited the old charges that Sherman was insane or on the edge of insanity. (Sherman spoke so much and his mind moved so rapidly that it was easier to remember what he had not said during an evening than what he had said.) In this instance, Sherman did not succeed in getting Knox hanged, but was able to have him permanently barred from the front.

Following his meeting with Cameron in Kentucky, Sherman had asked to be relieved of command, and was transferred to St Louis, where he soon asked leave to go home and rest. His wife Ellen, daughter of his adoptive father Thomas Ewing, former first Secretary of the Interior, wrote to his brother John that he was in a 'morbid state of anxiety' in Louisville (a state she had seen him approach once before in civilian life in California), and voiced concern because of insanity in the family. Undoubtedly, Sherman had sustained some kind of mental collapse. He recovered, however, and returned to duty in St Louis subdued and apparently more serene.

Here departmental commander General Henry W Halleck, who knew Sherman before the war, recognized Sherman's special talent in military planning, and drew him into planning sessions for Grant's successful 1862 campaign against Forts Henry and Donelson. Halleck also placed him in command of the Cairo district, Grant's rear zone in these operations, from which position Sherman cooperated by sending troops to the front. After the forts fell, he joined Grant in the field with a division of volunteers.

Here his initial admiration for Grant grew into a devoted friendship, and under Grant's supervision, Sherman grew sure of himself. Grant soon came to consider Sherman the ablest man in his command and marked him for promotion; Sherman recognized that Grant's unshakable faith in himself somehow communicated itself to him with a transforming effect. At Shiloh, where Sherman's division of raw troops received the full force of the Confederates' surprise attack, this nervous man who had lost his command and nearly lost his mind in Kentucky was cool and at ease in the heat of battle, even after two horses were shot out from under him (he lost four altogether) and he was wounded in the hand. When Grant arrived to ask him how things were going, Sherman replied of his desperate situation that it

Left to right: Sherman, Sheridan and Grant.

was not too bad, but he needed ammunition. Grant replied that he had already ordered it, and cantered off. Much later Grant wrote of that day at Shiloh, 'I never deemed it important to stay long with Sherman.' The intimacy these two men shared under fire at Shiloh was to bind them together for the rest of the war.

Their stars rose together. Sherman was promoted to major general of volunteers on 1 May 1862, and persuaded Grant, who came in for considerable criticism for his command at Shiloh, not to resign. Much later Sherman was to remark, 'General Grant is a great general. I know him well. He stood by me when I was crazy and I stood by him when he was drunk; and now, sir, we stand by each other always.'

At Vicksburg Sherman commanded a corps of 32,000 men as part of Grant's initial thrust, and quickly restored his reputation after his nearly inevitable failure at Chickasaw Bluffs by proposing, and then cooperating with, General John A McClernand in the capture of Fort Hindman, Arkansas, on 4-12 January 1863. For his service

at Vicksburg Sherman was made brigadier general in the US Army.

When Grant was placed in supreme command of the West, Sherman succeeded him as commander of the Army of the Tennessee. He was soon called upon by Grant to join in the rescue of besieged Union forces at Chattanooga, where he held the left flank against fierce assaults while General George H Thomas swept to victory on Missionary Ridge (24-5 November 1863). This was the last time Sherman and Grant were to fight together.

When Grant moved east to become commander of all Union armies, Sherman was appointed to top command in the West. In the spring of 1864 his command of over 100,000 men including George H Thomas's Army of the Cumberland (representing one half of his total forces); his old Army of the Tennessee, now led by brilliant young General James B McPherson; and the much smaller Army of the Ohio, really no more than a corps, led by General John Schofield. Encamped around Chattanooga, as prepared and ready for action as the enormous resources of the North and Sherman's fertile imagination could make them, these three armies awaited the signal from General Grant that would embark them on one of the major offensives calculated to break the back of the Confederacy.

The instructions that finally arrived from Grant ordered Sherman 'to move against Johnston's Army, to break it up, and to get into the interior of the enemy's country as far as you can, inflicting all the damage you can against their war resources.' Sherman was to head down the Western and Atlantic Railroad to the critical supply, manufacturing, and communications center of Atlanta, but as he himself remarked after the war, 'I was to go for Joe Johnston,' no holds barred. After Shiloh, both Grant and Sherman had come to the decision that ruthlessness was the only way to end this war.

Confederate commander Joe Johnston was well aware that his army of 60,000 could neither immediately take the offensive nor expect to defeat Sherman's superior forces in open battle,

and equally aware of the political considerations attendant on Sherman's advance. The war was not going well for the Union in the East. The Federals had not won a major battle since Chattanooga, and a growing war-weariness in the North had enabled the Democratic Party, led by presidential challenger General George B McClellan, to make vague promises of withdrawing from the war, or of otherwise accommodating the South. Johnston knew that a decisive Union victory was virtually the only hope for the reelection of Abraham Lincoln and the continuity of the war effort on its present scale. He realized that his tactics must therefore be Fabian, fighting in retreat, so to speak, in successive small battles that might lead Sherman to overextend his supply line and reduce his ability to protect it. Once he was thus weakened, Johnston would find an opportunity to strike with full force. By this tactic Johnston hoped at least to prevent Atlanta from falling before the Federal presidential election.

On 7 May 1864, three days after Grant marched out to do battle with Lee in the Wilderness, Sherman began his great offensive. That morning Union troops clashed with the enemy near Ringgold, Georgia. Johnston's position at Dalton was too strong to attack. In a pattern that was to be repeated again and again during the seventeen weeks of his 140-mile thrust to Atlanta, Sherman confronted the Confederates with Thomas's Army of the Cumberland and sent McPherson's and Schofield's armies on wide flanking maneuvers, forcing Johnston to withdraw. After four days of skirmishing, Johnston fell back to Resaca, one of nine successive defensive positions he would take up and abandon as he and Sherman engaged in a highly formal and deadly dance, Johnston never quite finding the conditions he wanted to make a decisive stand, and Sherman never quite able to trap this defensive specialist in the open.

Left: Former Major-General George B McClellan ran for president in 1864 on a peace platform.

Right: General Sherman's men destroy railroad tracks in their march to the sea.

Below: The cavalry battle at Trevilian Station, 12 June 1864.

As they fell back toward Atlanta, Johnston proved to be a master counterpuncher. Sherman had superior numbers and seldom made mistakes, but Johnston left no overextended flank or careless defense unmolested. Every day the armies were in contact, and casualties mounted up, but unlike the all-consuming fighting going on in Virginia that year, it was a chessboard campaign, with few pitched battles.

On 12 May Sherman mounted three futile attacks against the Rebel lines at Resaca, at the same time sending other forces around Johnston's left flank, in three days forcing the Confederates, without haste, to withdraw. Resaca was the real beginning of this extraordinary campaign. From then on the fighting was constant as both sides followed the railroad from Dalton to Atlanta, the Rebels breaking it up as they withdrew, the Yankees repairing it as they advanced. At Cassville, where his forces were concentrated against an ever widening Federal front, Johnston prepared to mount an attack, but was dissuaded by Generals John Bell Hood and Bishop Leonidas Polk, who claimed they were flanked. During the night of 19-20 May Johnston retired to Allatoona Pass, a position Sherman found too strong to assault, but once again flanked successfully after giving his army a three-day rest. Johnston sent cavalry under Nathan Bedford Forrest and Joseph Wheeler to raid Sherman's lengthening supply line.

On 25-7 May the first major fighting of the campaign took place at the hamlet of New Hope Church (Dallas). After both sides suffered significant but indecisive losses, Sherman moved east again, forcing Johnston to abandon his position and take up a new one to protect the railroad, a few miles northwest of Marietta. Here the Confederate corps commander, Leonidas Polk, an Episcopalian bishop and a guiding light of Johnston's army, was killed instantly by a Union cannonball as he reconnoitered from Pine Mountain. Johnston withdrew to prepared positions at Kennesaw Mountain. Thus far the fighting had accounted for about 9000 casualties on both sides, although Johnston's army, picking up reinforcements along the way, was actually larger by the time they reached Atlanta.

Early in June Sherman sent Federal cavalry under General S D Sturgis to deal with Nathan Forrest and other Confederate cavalry raiding his supply lines. On this occasion, the brilliant Forrest, outnumbered more than two to one, completely routed the Federals and inflicted enormous losses at Brice's Cross Roads, Mississippi, on 10 June. Federal efforts to hunt down Forrest would continue to fail right up to the end of the war, but so complete was Sherman's planning that these Confederate forays against his communications were more annoying than decisive, and did not hinder his advance.

Although he could have flanked Johnston again to destroy his position on Kennesaw Mountain, Sherman decided, perhaps because he

heard his troops were grumbling about too much marching, to make a frontal assault. On 27 June he sent picked divisions from Thomas's army against secure Confederate positions, and watched his men get blown to bits. A Rebel defender later wrote, 'I will ever think that the reason they did not capture our works was the impossibility of their living men to pass over the bodies of their dead.' Almost 3000 Federals died to 442 Rebels. As Grant had learned three weeks earlier at Cold Harbor, well-dug-in Confederates were impervious to frontal attack. Thomas remarked to Sherman, 'One or two more such assaults would use up this army.'

Sherman returned to his flanking tactics. Johnston, in his first serious mistake of the campaign, failed to anticipate McPherson's sweep around his right toward the Chattahoochee

Top left: General Sherman directs the costly battle at Kennesaw Mountain, 4 October 1864.

Above left: Major General Grenville Mellen Dodge, whose XVI Corps held back a Rebel attack on McPherson's flank at the Battle of Atlanta on 22 July 1864.

River, and as a result was forced to fall back precipitously to the river banks on the edge of Atlanta. By 9 July his men were in the trenches around Atlanta itself. Although he had conducted a model campaign and still had Atlanta to fall back on, which he had every reason to believe he could hold until after the Federal elections (Lincoln had by now privately recorded that he did not think he would be re-elected), Johnston's commander-in-chief neither understood nor was satisfied with his strategy. On 17 July Jefferson Davis replaced Johnston with John Bell Hood, an act that depressed the Confederate army and, as Sherman later wrote, 'rendered us most valuable service.' Sherman knew he would have no trouble compelling the pugnacious Hood to fight. He also knew that Hood was not of the stuff that makes for masterful command.

Crossing the Chattahoochee, Sherman closed in on Atlanta from the north and east. He had no intention of attacking the formidable earthworks that ringed Atlanta, but hoped to cut the four railroad lines converging on the city and thus compel the Rebels to flee or to fight in the open. With Schofield between the wings and McPherson executing a wide envelopment from the direction of Decatur, Thomas crossed Peachtree Creek from the north. Sherman had in fact incautiously left an opening – McPherson and Schofield with almost half the Federal troops were on the Georgia railroad, east of the city – and Hood, hoping to destroy Thomas before Sherman could reunite his forces, attacked him savagely at Peachtree Creek. It was an eventuality Johnston had anticipated and planned for. Unfortunately for Hood, Thomas and his men were at their best in defensive fighting. Hood's attack of 20 July was beaten off with considerable losses (4800 Confederate casualties to 1800 for the Union), and Thomas's army was able to re-establish contact with McPherson and Schofield.

When Hood withdrew into the defenses of Atlanta, Sherman erroneously concluded that he was abandoning the city. McPherson issued orders to move 'in pursuit to the south and east of Atlanta,' but Hood's cavalrymen reported McPherson's incautiously exposed flank, and Hood went after him. This flank attack of 22 July, resulting in the fight known as the Battle of Atlanta, came fairly close to a Confederate success. McPherson, who had been conferring with Sherman and rode off to take a look at the sound of shooting, was killed at its commencement. Sherman wept unashamedly when his body was brought back to headquarters. For a time the Army of the Tennessee was assailed brutally from both front and rear, but due largely to the fortuitous presence of General Grenville Dodge's XVI Corps, the Confederate onslaught was stopped, and Hood had to pull his men back inside their fortified lines.

Confederate casualties for the two days of fighting were about 13,000 to the Union's 5500. Sherman successfully cut the railroads that came into Atlanta from the north and east, but also missed a major opportunity. He had refused to reinforce the Army of the Tennessee so that the Army of the Cumberland would be ready to move on Atlanta, which was defended by only one Rebel corps as Hood massed everything else against McPherson, but he had waited too long. Brilliant a strategist as he was, Sherman was not yet the complete master of battlefield tactics, and the chance to capture Atlanta then and there was lost.

By 25 July Sherman had invested Atlanta on the north and east. Pulling the Army of the Tennessee, now under General Oliver Otis Howard, out of line, he sent it behind his other armies in a wide arc east to west to cut the Macon and Western railroad to the south. Hood came out to meet him at Ezra Church (25 July) where his army again suffered considerable losses in six assault waves that failed to rout the Yankees, but succeeded in keeping the railroad open. Sherman sent 10,000 cavalry under Edward McCook and George Stoneman to raid Macon and cut the railroad; Stoneman's division was all but wiped out and McCook's was routed and dispersed.

At last controlling all but one railroad into the city, at the end of July Sherman settled down to besiege Atlanta, investing the city on three sides and slowly extending his lines. Kennesaw Mountain had taught him that frontal assaults against strong Confederate fortifications were useless. Although he had a two-to-one manpower advantage and had been unable to destroy Hood's army, he began to realize that the campaign could still be a success if he took Atlanta, particularly with respect to the political effect it would have

on the North, where Lincoln's re-election became daily more questionable.

Hood gave Sherman the opening he had been waiting for by sending Wheeler's cavalry to the north on a month-long raid on Sherman's communications, 10 August-10 September. But Sherman had already collected all the supplies he needed, and he further realized that the absence of cavalry weakened the Confederate position in Atlanta. On 26 August, leaving only a small force before the city, Sherman pulled Schofield and Thomas out of their trenches and made a wide sweep west around Atlanta. Hood, misinterpreting this move, concluded he was giving up, and sent troops south to Jonesboro to hurry him on his route.

The Federals easily repulsed them, and by midnight of 31 August Schofield and Thomas had cut Hood's remaining railroad at two places. Realizing the game was up, Hood evacuated Atlanta on 1 September, blowing up munitions and stores before heading for entrenchments to the southwest at Lovejoy. Sherman wired Lincoln on 2 September, 'Atlanta is ours, and fairly won.' Lincoln, rejoicing over his greatly improved prospects for re-election, declared a national day of celebration for the victories of Atlanta and Mobile Bay (5 August), and in the North public confidence in ultimate victory was reborn.

Sherman was by now less interested in Hood's army than in destroying Georgia's will and capacity for war, which he proposed to accomplish by bringing the full weight of the war to bear on the Confederate civilians. Although he had failed to destroy Hood's army, as the war had progressed and his thinking evolved – he would eventually be called the 'Prophet of Total War' – Hood seemed to matter less and less. Sherman pursued him to Lovejoy, where he found his position too strong to assault, and ordered all Union troops

Top: An etching that appeared in the 10 December 1864 issue of *Frank Leslie's Illustrated Newspaper*, depicting soldiers being paid off in Atlanta before the commencement of the march across the southern states.

Above: Sherman's men destroying railroad tracks in Atlanta.

back to Atlanta early in September to consolidate his gains.

Before setting out on the campaign that was now about to turn into an exemplary demonstration of his concept of total war, Sherman had remarked, 'War, like the thunderbolt, follows its laws and turns not aside even if the beautiful, the virtuous and the charitable stand in its path.' His first step in Atlanta, which he proposed to turn into a military camp, was to order the evacuation, forcible if necessary, of all its citizens. To their protests he replied, 'You might as well appeal against the thunderstorm as against these terrible hardships of war.' To Halleck he wrote, 'If the people raise a howl against my barbarity and cruelty, I will answer that war is war, and not popularity seeking. If they want peace, they and their relations must stop the war.'

Sherman had an extended argument over the telegraph wires with Grant on his proposed march from Atlanta to the sea. Grant felt it would be wise to dispose of Hood before going off on a new campaign, was not sure Thomas could handle him alone, and felt that the navy ought to seize and prepare some seaport city as a base before Sherman moved east. Sherman, however, held fast to his conviction that nothing would hasten the end of the war so much as the demonstration that a Union army could go anywhere it chose in the Confederacy.

Grant finally agreed. The campaign that was to have the strongest psychological impact of any in the war was justified by Sherman in a letter to Halleck: 'As a nation the United States has the right, and also the physical power to penetrate to every part of the national domain ... [to] take every life, every acre of land, every particle of property ... until the end is attained.' On another occasion he wrote, 'I can make the march, and make Georgia howl.'

On 8 November Abraham Lincoln was re-elected President of the United States. A week later, ordering his army to live off the land and to 'enforce a devastation more or less relentless,' Sherman cut his supply lines and left Atlanta in flames. He had ordered the destruction only of factories, warehouses, railroad installations and such property as might be of use to the Confederacy, with fires to be set only when he was present; but most of the city was by now uninhabited and his soldiers were careless with matches, with the result that most of the city went up in smoke.

Sherman's 56,000 infantry, 5000 cavalry, and 2000 artillerymen were organized into two wings – the right, the Army of the Tennessee, under General Oliver Howard; and the left, the so-called Army of Georgia, under General Henry Slocum. The wings marched from Atlanta in

A dreary forced march of Confederate prisoners being conducted to Atlanta from Jonesboro.

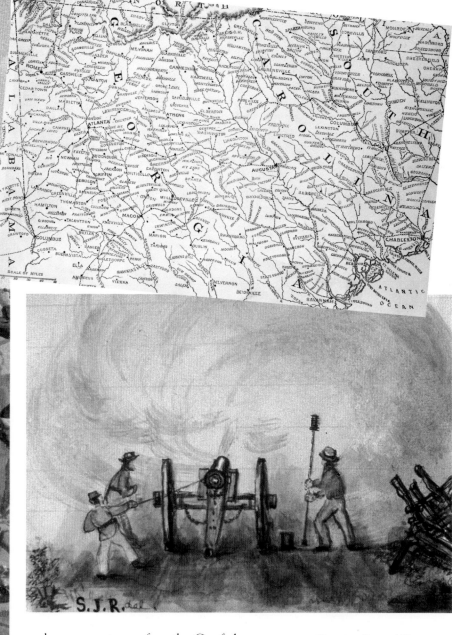

such a way as to confuse the Confederates as to whether their true objective was Macon, Augusta, or Savannah. Although there would be some resistance from a motley collection of Georgia militia and Wheeler's cavalry, this Confederate force of 13,000 was never more than an annoyance. Sherman's cavalry handled most of the limited fighting of the campaign.

For the soldiers the march was more like a prolonged, rowdy picnic than a regular war. Their instructions were to average a leisurely fifteen miles per day while laying waste a bountiful Georgia countryside fat from fall harvests, doing as much harm to the Confederate warmaking machine as possible, demonstrating to the world that the Confederacy could not protect the homes, property or families of its own defenders; in short, to destroy the spirit of the Confederate nation, to destroy a faith that the Confederacy was an enduring creation that could protect and avenge its people. The army spread out to cover a front of sixty miles, systematically devastating a 250-mile strip of some of the richest farmland in the South.

Strictly speaking, each brigade sent out 20 to

Opposite: General Sherman oversees the artillery bombardment in the siege of Atlanta, 9 August 1864.

Top: A map depicting Sherman's advance into northern Georgia.

Above: Samuel J Reader's *Glimpse of a Shell.*

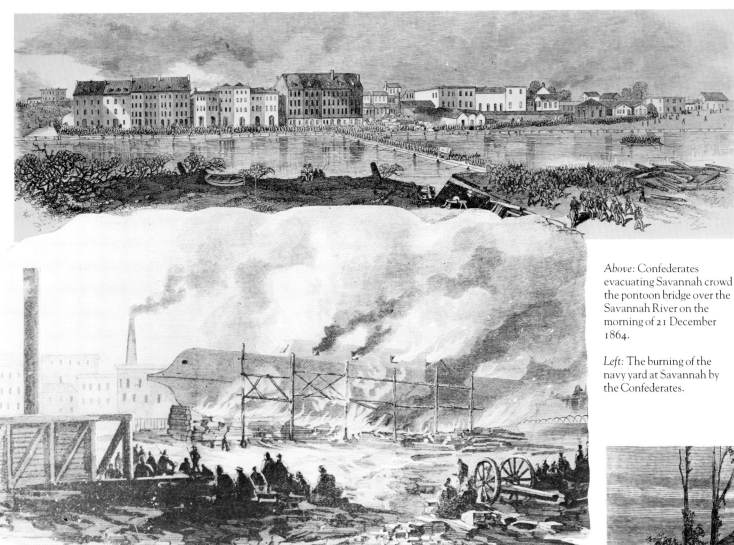

Above: Confederates evacuating Savannah crowd the pontoon bridge over the Savannah River on the morning of 21 December 1864.

Left: The burning of the navy yard at Savannah by the Confederates.

50 foragers each day, but as a practical matter most soldiers foraged constantly. Hordes of homeless slaves followed the Federals, many sharing in a take of food so overabundant that it appalled many of the soldiers. Sherman later estimated that his army caused $100 million worth of damage in Georgia, $20 million representing material his army actually used, and the rest 'simple waste and destruction.' As it marched the army was preceded, surrounded, and followed by a destructive horde of lawless stragglers called 'bummers.' These were deserters, AWOLs, and brigands of all kinds, both Federal and Confederate, who robbed, pillaged, and burned all the way from Atlanta to the sea, outside of any controls.

On 10 December Sherman surfaced on the coast just below Savannah, where he took Fort McAllister at the mouth of the Ogeechee River and made contact with the Federal fleet. While news of his safe arrival sped North, Sherman prepared to take Savannah and the force of 10,000 that had been gathered to defend it. To Savannah's commanding Confederate General William S Hardee Sherman wrote, 'Should I be forced to assault . . . I shall then feel justified in resorting to the harshest measures and shall make little effort to restrain my army.' Sherman pro-

ceeded to bring up siege guns, but Hardee managed to get his garrison out safely into South Carolina. Sherman's men marched into Savannah on 21 December. On 24 December Sherman wired to Lincoln, 'I beg to present you, as a Christmas gift, the city of Savannah,' a gift which included 25,000 bales of cotton and considerable materiel.

Ten days previous to the fall of Savannah Hood's forces had been effectively destroyed as a fighting force by Sherman's army under Thomas at Nashville. With the Confederate Army of Tennessee shattered and the Confederacy definitively cut in two, Sherman's offensives of 1864 in the South were immeasurably effective. Newspapers that had once called him crazy now called him 'Tecumseh the Great,' and his men, who had long before succumbed to his paternalistic streak and viewed him with a peculiarly possessive affection, vowed to follow 'Uncle Billy' to the ends of the earth. Suffering fewer than 2200 casualties, Sherman had destroyed a large portion of the South's war potential in Georgia, and was in a position to co-operate effectively with Grant's forces in Virginia. At the beginning of 1865, due in part to his efforts, all of the Confederacy left to be reckoned with consisted of the Carolinas and southern Virginia.

Shortly after the beginning of the new year,

Sherman continued his march of destruction into the Carolinas. While essentially the same sort of operation as the March to the Sea, it was decidedly different in tone. In Georgia his soldiers had destroyed for the fun of it, without any particular animosity; in South Carolina, the birthplace of secession, they acted with vengeance. They were convinced that shattering South Carolina would grind out the South's will to resist. In South Carolina Sherman's army destroyed literally everything in its path. Charleston fell without a shot, and Columbia, South Carolina's capital, went up in flames. By the time the Federals swarmed into North Carolina, soldiers were deserting Lee's army in droves to protect their homesteads. On 16 March Confederate troops under Hardee tried to stem the tide at Averysboro; three days later, in the largest engagement of the campaign, Joe Johnston, once more in charge of the Army of Tennessee, tried again at Bentonville. Sherman did not press his advantage. A month later, on 17 April 1865, eight days after Lee's surrender at Appomattox, Johnston and Sherman met in a farmhouse in Raleigh, North Carolina, to complete the terms of Johnston's surrender. On his way to that farmhouse, Sherman had been handed a telegram telling him of the assassination of Lincoln. He said nothing of it to anyone until he was alone with Johnston, when he handed over the telegram for him to read. The defeated Confederate received the news with obvious emotion, pronouncing it, in accurate prophecy, 'the greatest possible calamity to the South.'

The terms of surrender Sherman offered were essentially those of the Grant-Lee agreement, although broader and rather more liberal, to the astonishment of Washington and the Northern press. Secretary of War Stanton, assuming a dictatorial role in a nation shocked by Lincoln's death, and believing the assassination to be a deliberate Confederate plot, called Sherman disloyal or crazy. Sherman, quite properly outraged, claimed that he was fully aware of what Lincoln's intentions had been, and in the controversy that followed nearly ruined his career trying to befriend the South. With the passage of time and his inevitable enshrinement in the North as an unstained hero and in the South as an unmitigated monster, few would remember his efforts at reconciliation. One who did was General Joe Johnston, who lived long enough to die of pneumonia contracted while standing hatless in the rain at Sherman's funeral.

Union troops halt for a rest in their penetration of the South, as depicted by artist Thomas Nast.

PHILIP SHERIDAN

Shenandoah Valley Campaign
Siege of Petersburg

The fall of Petersburg.

The purpose of fighting battles and wars is, of course, to win them, and there are those who contend that any means tending to achieve that end is acceptable. Some great generals, such as Lee and Grant and Jackson, gain victory and glory by exceptional tactical or strategic skills; others seem to forge their place in history by sheer fight and force of will. 'Little Phil' Sheridan is of the latter type: he was sometimes outmaneuvered, but never outfought. Even when his army had been scattered in panic, the galvanizing presence of Sheridan riding over the battlefield seemed able to turn defeat into victory. For good reason one of his generals described him as, 'that storm center spirit, that form of condensed energies.' Not that Sheridan lacked either brains or tactical skills, only that he usually won the day whether his tactics succeeded or not.

Sheridan was born to Irish immigrant parents in Albany, New York, on 6 March 1831, his family soon moving to Somerset, Ohio. He spent an uneventful boyhood there; any evidence of exceptional ability was far in the future. As a

Philip Henry Sheridan (1831-1888), whose aggressive tactics in battle brought victory and facilitated his rise from lieutenant to full general and commander-in-chief of the US Army.

youth he worked as a bookkeeper in country stores; meanwhile, a determination to be a soldier formed in his mind, perhaps that being his only ticket out of small-town Ohio. Finally he wangled from his congressman an appointment to the US Military Academy, reporting to West Point in June of 1848.

At the Academy Sheridan was far from a model student, though he showed enough enterprise to avoid flunking by studying nights after lights were out with his roommate as tutor. In his senior year he demonstrated his pugnacity and in the process nearly ended his military career: displeased by the tone of an order, he broke ranks and took out after a cadet officer with a bayonet. But apparently he had impressed someone enough to earn a second chance; after a year's suspension he was readmitted and graduated with the class of 1853, 34th in a class of 52.

There followed eight years of Indian fighting as an infantry lieutenant in the West and Northwest. How well he did in that service is indicated by the fact that when the Civil War broke out he was still a lieutenant, a rather old one at 30, wondering when and how he was going to get to fight and, more important, be promoted.

Sheridan's first efforts during the war were just as unpromising as his previous career, though he was made a captain in May 1861. Maybe because of his youthful bookkeeping experience, he became a quartermaster for Union troops in Missouri. He was rescued by General Halleck, who was on his way to Corinth, Mississippi, in the aftermath of the battle of Shiloh. Halleck made Sheridan his quartermaster, and Sheridan measured up to the requirements in that unadventurous service. But he yearned for action. In May 1862 he got his chance, becoming colonel of the 2nd Michigan Cavalry, and soon he commanded a brigade. One month later came the day that started his star rising.

On 1 July 1862 some 5000 Rebel cavalry attacked Sheridan's brigade of 827 at Booneville, Mississippi. A withdrawal seemed inevitable, and Sheridan was so authorized. Instead he attacked, working a few men onto the rear and flank of the Confederates and surprising them into a rout. As of that day he was promoted to brigadier general of volunteers, and a superior wrote to Halleck of Sheridan, 'He is worth his weight in gold.' (That weight happened to be all of 115 lbs, carried within a 5'5" frame. He had a lot of compensating to do to make up for his size, and did so with a vengeance.)

On the first of October 1862 Sheridan took command of a division in Don Carlos Buell's Army of the Ohio. Eight days later he was leading his troops in fighting at Perryville, Kentucky. Confederate assaults had shaken the Federals there in a confused and bloody afternoon of battle when Sheridan's division, holding the keypoint of the Union line, threw back an attack and then counterattacked, driving the Rebels back through Perryville. Sheridan had helped turn a dangerous situation into a victory, though one Buell failed to exploit, and that clinched the acclaim he had gained at Booneville.

The end of 1862 found Sheridan serving under Rosecrans's Army of the Cumberland in Murfreesboro, Tennessee. On 31 December Southern forces under General Braxton Bragg battered the Federals at Stone's River, but Sheridan doggedly held onto his position, turning away four enemy charges, and then routed the oncoming Rebels with practically no ammunition. That battle ended indecisively, but Rosecrans was happy enough about Sheridan's performance to make him a major general of volunteers.

At Chickamauga, Georgia, on 20 September 1863, the Army of the Cumberland could not stop Bragg's forces. Sheridan was brushed aside when the enemy smashed Rosecrans's line; he and his men were lucky to make it back to Chattanooga in one piece along with most of the Federal army. Then, in late November, the Army of the Cumberland, now under U S Grant, got its revenge. Led by Sheridan's division, the Federals charged up Missionary Ridge and sent Bragg running back into Georgia. Sheridan came within an ace of capturing Bragg himself, and his was the only element of the Union forces to mount an organized pursuit.

That extraordinary victory changed the course of Union strategy and the careers of Grant and Sheridan. Given overall command of Union armies in March 1864, Grant told Lincoln and Halleck he wanted 'the very best man in the army' for his cavalry commander. 'How would Sheridan do?' Halleck suggested. 'The very man I want,' replied Grant.

Sheridan was virtually unknown in the East, an infantry leader called in to command the huge cavalry of the Army of the Potomac – three divisions, some 10,000 troopers and six batteries of horse artillery. In his *Memoirs* Sheridan recalled a scarifying interview with imperious War Secretary Edwin Stanton, who seemed dubious about a bandy-legged little Irishman of 33 years being given the most important cavalry position in the army. But Sheridan noted, 'his frequent commendation in after years indicated that I gained his good-will before the close of the war, if not when I first came to his notice.'

Soon Grant had developed a broad strategy to win the war. Meanwhile Sheridan completely organized the cavalry and formed his own convictions about how to use it. Under General George Meade and earlier commanders of the Army of the Potomac, the cavalry had been spread out in horse-killing picket duty and largely nursemaid services; thus the old infantry jibe, 'Who ever saw a dead cavalryman?' Sheridan was determined to make his command into a compact fighting force, for his cavalry to fight Jeb Stuart's. 'I'm going to take the cavalry away from the bobtailed brigadier generals,' he proclaimed. 'They must do without their escorts.' When confronted with this notion Meade responded with dismay, but did agree to take the cavalry off picket duty.

Soon Sheridan had gotten his divisions in fighting trim, and the troopers had decided that they rather liked this new man. They found that if they did their jobs he would treat them very well indeed – he was more attentive to food supplies than most generals. If they ran afoul of

General Philip Sheridan and staff. Left to right: Sheridan, Colonel James Forsythe, General Wesley Merritt, Thomas C Devin and George A Custer.

Left: In the spectacular Union capture of Lookout Mountain at Chattanooga on 23 November 1863, General Sheridan played a key role.

Below: Federal forces charge at the Battle of the Wilderness, fought on the 5th and 6th of May 1864. Because of the thick, smoke-filled woods, much of the battle was fought in utter confusion, regiments losing contact with one another and men grappling at point blank range.

Sheridan, however, they were apt to be shipped out to where life was tougher, or at least to endure one of his famous tirades. In an army that marched and fought by swear-power as much as anything else, Sheridan still elicited awe with his mastery of malediction.

Marching south with Meade at the beginning of May 1864, Grant took the Army of the Potomac straight toward Richmond, knowing that Robert E Lee would show up somewhere. That proved to be in the thickets of the Virginia Wilderness, where Lee's Army of Northern Virginia jumped Grant's column and in two days of terrible fighting came close to ending Grant's game at the outset. Instead of turning tail as his predecessors had done, Grant slipped around Lee and headed for Richmond again, Lee moving to stop him.

During the ensuing footrace that was to end in battle at Spotsylvania, Union cavalry and infantry stumbled over one another on the roads, Meade and Sheridan issuing contradictory orders to the troopers. That led to a shouting match between Meade and Sheridan on 8 May. Finally Meade stormed off to complain to Grant, mentioning that this upstart had even claimed he could whip Jeb Stuart. Grant went right to the heart of the issue: 'Did Sheridan say that? Well, he generally knows what he is talking about. Let him start right out and do it.' Thus began Sheridan's Richmond Raid, which did not make it quite to Richmond but nonetheless paid off handsomely. The fiery Union cavalryman and his debonair Southern opponent were well matched.

With 10,000 troopers and artillery, three divisions under Wesley Merritt, David Gregg, and James Wilson, Sheridan set off on 9 May in the

Left: The battle at the vital Confederate crossroads of Spotsylvania took place in May 1864. After an argument in which Meade blamed the cavalry for impeding ground forces, Sheridan took the cavalry on a raid around Lee's army to disrupt supply lines.

Constant pursuit and fighting characterized the way from Five Forks to Appomattox, as depicted in this drawing by R F Zogbaum.

general direction of Richmond, knowing Jeb Stuart would be sure to contest his march. That day and the next a Southern rail junction at Beaver Dam Station was wrecked by a hard-fighting young Union general named George Armstrong Custer, who was to become a particular favorite of Sheridan's.

Stuart was not long in taking the bait, sending a column to harass Sheridan's rear. By 11 May Stuart realized he had better get between these Yankees and his capital, and with about 1100 men rode hurriedly to intercept the enemy column at a little road-crossing called Yellow Tavern. Sheridan's advance arrived at Yellow Tavern before noon on 11 May and began a few probing attacks, the men exercising their Spencer repeating carbines to push back Stuart's left. A lull followed, during which more of Sheridan's troopers arrived, and about four o'clock Federal bugles sounded the charge. Soon Stuart was pressed all along his line, and it began to crumble. In late afternoon Custer took some Michigan regiments forward to assault the shaken Rebel left flank.

Custer's men began at a walk, then changed gait to a trot, then pitched into the enemy at a full

run. The Confederates broke apart in dust and screaming, but a Virginia regiment appeared to drive Custer away. The Federals pulled back past a Confederate officer who sat on his horse directing his men. Union private John A Huff tried a potshot at the Rebel officer with his pistol and was gratified to see the man reel in the saddle. It is not recorded if Huff realized he had just shot Jeb Stuart, who was carried from the field mortally wounded. Soon the Yankee cavalry swept the Rebels from the field.

At Yellow Tavern Sheridan had engineered the first unequivocal Union cavalry victory of the war. Moreover, in killing Jeb Stuart, his men had also ended once and for all the ascendancy of the Southern cavalry. Now it would be the Union riders who would write the glorious chapters. Though the rest of his raid amounted to little – except terrifying Richmond when he nicked its defenses – Sheridan had accomplished his main objective, and Grant received him with appropriate acclaim when the riders returned in late May.

Soon came the debacle of Cold Harbor, where Grant threw his infantry at Lee's entrenchments and lost 7000 men to no purpose. After that

Left: General Barlow charges the enemy at Cold Harbor, 1 July 1864. After this debacle Grant headed for Petersburg.

Grant gave up his designs on Richmond and decided to pick up his army as quietly as possible and head for Petersburg, which was in effect the back door to the Confederate capital and the focal point of the railroads that were Richmond's lifeline. Wishing a diversion to cover his movement and hoping for some railroad-smashing, Grant sent Sheridan and the cavalry on a raid west. From the major engagement of the campaign this became known as the Trevilian Raid.

Sheridan left on 7 June 1864. On the 11th came the sharp fight at Trevilian Station, which Custer opened by impetuously assaulting the rear of Wade Hampton's cavalry without realizing that Fitz Lee's Rebel troopers were on *his* rear. Thus, after capturing a considerable haul of Rebels and supplies, Custer found himself trapped between two Southern columns, which closed in, recaptured their supplies, and pressed Custer's lines nearly into a circle.

Sheridan spent the rest of the day extricating Custer from this muddle at Trevilian Station, and a confusing time was had by all. Both sides claimed victory, but neither in the battle nor in the ensuing raid did Sheridan cause much damage to the South, though he did help screen Grant's movements. At the end of June an exhausted Sheridan was back with the Army of the Potomac, which was now besieging Petersburg. Sheridan brought a certain amount of captured supplies and prisoners, but was missing a good many men and a great many horses.

Despite the disappointment of the Trevilian Raid, Grant retained an unassailable faith in Sheridan. Thus came the most important assignment of Sheridan's career: to take a force of mixed infantry and cavalry, the Army of the Shenandoah, into the Shenandoah Valley.

Confederate cavalry officer John Singleton Mosby.

Confederate general Jubal Anderson Early.

Lying between the Blue Ridge Mountains to the east and the Alleghenies on the west, the Shenandoah spreads diagonally down the center of Virginia for over 100 miles, averaging some 25 miles in width. It is the most lovely and fertile land in the state, perhaps in the whole South. For the Confederacy it was a protected funnel leading to Maryland and the North for invasions, a safe return in retreat. It was also the granary of the South, food source of the Rebel armies. All over the Valley Confederate guerrillas pursued their hitting and running, most prominent among them the brilliant raider John Singleton Mosby, whose field of operations was known as 'Mosby's Confederacy.'

In 1864 Federal efforts to establish a presence in the Valley had been stymied primarily by a wily, white-bearded old Rebel general named Jubal Early, who in July had taken a group of raiders out of the Shenandoah right to the gates of

Federal forces led by Sheridan attack Early's Confederate troops at Winchester, or Opequon, on 19 September 1864.

Washington, causing no great harm but considerable panic. Grant had had enough of Early and Mosby and the easy flow of supplies from the Shenandoah to the South. He ordered Sheridan and the Army of the Shenandoah, 48,000 strong, to bring the Valley under Union control once and for all.

In the beginning of August Sheridan moved his army to the vicinity of Harper's Ferry, the northern gateway of the Shenandoah, and over the next weeks sparred with elements of Early's command. By the beginning of September Sheridan had not budged to speak of, and both Grant and Early drew their conclusions: Grant, that Sheridan was being uncharacteristically slow; Early, that this new Yankee general was the timid sort. Finally, on 16 September, Grant came to Sheridan with a plan in his pocket. It proved to

be unnecessary: Sheridan had his army ready now and had just heard what he was waiting for – that Early had let go a substantial force to join Lee at Petersburg. Now Sheridan outnumbered Early about three to one and was ready to attack. Grant approved Sheridan's plans and never again bothered to visit him to review a campaign.

On 17 September Early, still thinking he was facing an unenterprising opponent, moved north in the Valley to operate against Union railroads. Two days later Sheridan struck Early hard at Winchester, and nearly got himself whipped. Early had only 16,000 men to Sheridan's 43,000, but the Confederates were well entrenched and waiting for the Yankees.

This was Sheridan's first engagement at the head of a big army, and he made his share of mistakes. He had planned a double envelopment,

Top right: Sheridan's final charge at Winchester.

Right: Sheridan's army routes the Confederates at Fisher's Hill on 22 September 1864.

The decisive charge upon the Confederates at the stone wall at the Battle of Winchester, as depicted by A Waud.

his cavalry striking the enemy flanks while the infantry moved on the center. But his infantry was left unsupported in attacking the middle, supply lines had gotten snarled the day before the battle, and Early put up unexpected resistance. Despite these setbacks, Sheridan's strategy made its effect in the end. The bulk of his 9000 cavalrymen pressed hard on Early's flanks, the Southern horsemen were outnumbered and outfought, and Early's infantry was forced out of position by the presence of Yankee cavalry in the rear. Finally the Rebels were in full retreat through Winchester. Southern losses were some 3000 casualties and 2000 prisoners; the North lost 653 killed, 3719 wounded and 618 missing.

Sheridan had fought in what became his unique style, seeming to be all over the battlefield at once on his charger. He had needed some seasoning, and he got it at Winchester. There he learned the importance of co-operation between infantry and cavalry. It was to prove his edge throughout the campaign.

Though soundly defeated at Winchester, Early was far from having the fight knocked out of him. Under heavy pursuit from Union cavalry, the 12,000 remaining Confederates dug in on an uneven ridge called Fisher's Hill, near Middletown. Entrenched on high ground, Early felt confident of making a stand. He was in for a surprise. On the evening of 20 September Sheridan sent

George Crook's infantry marching around to the enemy left and rear, where they lay concealed in the woods throughout the next day while Sheridan prepared a bluff assault on Early's front.

In the Battle of Fisher's Hill on 22 September, Early found Crook attacking his front and left flank while Union cavalry under William Averell had moved around his right to the rear. Finally Sheridan led a general charge, bellowing, 'Forward everything!' General Early got out while the getting was good, losing only 240 casualties, but, more seriously, also losing twelve cannon and 1000 prisoners. He got away clean from the troops Sheridan sent in pursuit, though it was weeks before he was able to fight again. Mean-

while, and not for the last time, Sheridan broke one of his commanders for not moving fast enough – in this case William Averell, who had mounted only desultory pursuit of the retreating Confederates.

Having now whipped Jubal Early twice, Sheridan could turn to his second objective – ending the flow of food from the Valley to the Confederacy, and also showing the citizenry of the South what war was really like. As Sherman was shortly to demonstrate in Georgia as well, this was the beginning of what a later age would call Total War: an assault not only on the armies but on the whole people and territory and produce of the enemy country. 'If the war is to last,' Grant

John S Mosby and his Confederate raiders lay in ambush in the forest. Sheridan's cavalry were harassed by the raiders as they carried out their campaign of destruction.

Early was nearby at Strasburg. Furthermore, Sheridan had intercepted a message purporting to be to Early from Confederate General James Longstreet which said, 'Be ready to move as soon as my forces join you, and we will crush Sheridan.' Suspecting the message was a trick (as in fact it was), Sheridan was still uneasy, and hurried back from Washington to spend the night of the 18th at Winchester, 20 miles from Cedar Creek.

Next morning Sheridan was awakened by an orderly who reported firing in the distance, presumably from a Federal reconnaissance. Sheridan rushed through breakfast and set out toward Cedar Creek on his big black charger Rienzi. When he was about 14 miles from Cedar Creek, he began to hear steady firing. Puzzled, he dismounted and put his ear to the ground: he heard the rumble of cannon fire, the clatter of rifles. Mounting Rienzi again, he broke into a trot.

Riding over a crest near Cedar Creek, Sheridan found one of the most terrifying sights of his life. In his own words: 'a panic-stricken army – hundreds of slightly wounded men, throngs of others unhurt but utterly demoralized, and baggage-wagons by the score, all pressing to the rear in hopeless confusion, telling only too plainly that a disaster had occurred at the front. On accosting some of the fugitives, they assured me that the army was broken up, in full retreat, and that all was lost.' Ringing in Sheridan's mind over and over during the next desperate hours was Longstreet's message, 'Be ready when I join you, and we will crush Sheridan.'

Longstreet was not there, but Early had jumped the Federal camp in the early morning fog, sending most of the Yankees out of their tents and running in panic to the rear. Looking at the chaos a few hours later, Sheridan decided that the situation still might be salvageable; after all, the rear of an army usually looks like a rout. Soon Sheridan learned that the VI Corps was mounting resistance near the Union camp, slowing the Confederate advance. Meanwhile the majority of the army were not running any more but calmly making coffee in the fields and waiting for someone to figure out what to do – by now these men were about as professional as soldiers can be and were used to victories. Spurring Rienzi into a gallop, Sheridan bolted forward into his men, waving his hat. As they caught sight of him the men burst into cheers.

By his own account he told the men, 'If I had been with you this morning, this disaster would not have happened. We must face the other way; we will go back and recover our camp.' An eyewitness report is probably more accurate: redfaced Little Phil, in full battle frenzy, rode back and forth bellowing over and over, 'God damn you, don't cheer me! If you love your country, come up to the front! God *damn* you, don't cheer me! There's lots of fight in you men yet! Come up, God damn you, come up!' Despite the invective the men kept cheering their commander, but they came up too. As a weary officer told his men,

wrote to Sheridan, 'we want the Shenandoah Valley to remain a barren waste.' Sheridan's task was to make a bountiful and beautiful territory into a wasteland, and Grant knew he was the man to do it.

On 6 October Sheridan began withdrawing to the northeast, his route marked by burning barns, houses, crops, and mills, by weeping farmers and their wives and children. To Grant Sheridan reported, 'I have destroyed over 2000 barns filled with wheat, hay, and farming implements; over 70 mills filled with flour and wheat; have driven in front of the army over four herd of stock, and have killed not less than 3000 sheep. A large number of horses have been obtained. My engineer officer was murdered [by partisans] beyond Harrisonburg. For this atrocious act all the houses within an area of five miles were burned.'

Sheridan's troops, mostly the cavalry, skirmished constantly with Mosby and other partisans and with Early's riders. Occasionally partisans were caught, sometimes they were hanged or shot, sometimes their relatives were arrested. It was a dirty, demoralizing way to fight a war, much of it against helpless farmers and terrified women and children, and many of the Northern soldiers had no taste for it; battle seemed clean and innocent by comparison. But the barns had to be burned all the same, that was their orders.

By October Sheridan was weary of being picked at by Confederate riders and testily ordered his cavalry commander, A T A Torbert, to 'whip the enemy or be whipped yourself.' On 9 October Torbert did as ordered at Tom's Brook. In a brisk fight on horseback, both sides went from carbines to pistols to sabers before the Confederates were routed with Federals close behind. Their 20-mile pursuit came to be known as the 'Woodstock Races.'

On 16 October Sheridan left for Washington to consult with Lincoln and Stanton. Though things seemed calmer after the Rebel humiliation at Tom's Brook, he was reluctant to leave; his army was camped at Cedar Creek, and he knew

'We may as well do it now; Sheridan will get it out of us some time.' Men began kicking over their coffee and picking up their guns; regiments formed, then divisions, and then they were an army again, heading back toward the enemy.

It took five hours of painstaking work, while Early entrenched, for Sheridan to organize his counterattack. At two o'clock the Confederates tried an attack that got nowhere. Many Southerners had remained in the Yankee camps, looting and helping themselves to whiskey. In late afternoon Sheridan rode the length of his line shouting 'We've got the goddamdest twist on them you ever saw!' Then 200 bugles bleated the charge, and the Union infantry and cavalry pitched into the Rebels.

A dramatic depiction of Sheridan's 20-mile ride from Winchester to the battle at Cedar Creek, where he reorganized his chaotic and panic-stricken forces.

A cavalry charge struck the Southern flanks; a man on the wrong side of that charge later recalled it: 'There came from the north side of the plain, a dull heavy swelling sound like a roaring of a distant cyclone, the omen of additional disaster. It was unmistakable. Sheridan's horsemen [it was Custer and his division] riding furiously across the open fields of grass to intercept the Confederates. . . . The only possiblity of saving the rear regiments was in unrestrained flight – every man for himself.'

Early's army broke apart and fled back through the Federal camps and away into the ravaged Shenandoah, this time too stricken to be a threat again. That day at Cedar Creek was the last organized Confederate resistance in the Valley, though Mosby would remain active to the end of the war. In February of 1865 George Custer put the final touch on the Shenandoah Valley Campaign when his horsemen annihilated Early's last remaining force at Waynesboro. The beautiful Valley Stonewall Jackson had, less than three

Right: The scene of the explosion in the Petersburg mine assault. Federal forces, by means of a 511-foot underground tunnel loaded with powder, blew a huge crater in the southern position through which to attack, but were decisively rebuffed.

Below: Petersburg, Virginia.

years earlier, fought so hard and successfully to protect and preserve, was now so barren that, as Sheridan himself gleefully reported, even a crow flying over it would have to take its rations with it.

Now a major general in the regular army, Sheridan joined Grant at Petersburg for the final act of the great drama. By this time Lee's once triumphant Army of Northern Virginia was starved and exhausted, decimated by death and desertion, and ready for the kill. With Sheridan as his spearhead, Grant cut three railroads and two canals and destroyed Southern supply depots. The Rebels began calling their tormentor 'Sheridan the inevitable': wherever they went or wanted to go, Sheridan seemed to be there waiting for them.

At the end of March 1865 a desperate Lee sent General George Pickett to drive Grant away from the last two railroads leading to Petersburg and Richmond, and to keep open an avenue of retreat. For a few nerve-racking days Federal forces bogged down in heavy rain and mud while Sheridan raged in his tent, 'I tell you, I'm ready to strike out tomorrow and go to smashing things!' On 1 April Sheridan got his chance; he wrecked Pickett's force at Five Forks, capturing 6000 ragged and hungry Rebels. During the battle Sheridan rode about the front waving a guidon and shouting his men on (he also cashiered one of his generals on the spot for being too slow). That loss forced Lee to pull out of Petersburg the night of 2 April and endeavor to retreat to the west in hope of joining the only other operating Con-federate army, in North Carolina.

At Appomattox on 9 April Sheridan's men captured four trains that held Lee's last rations. Surrounded, Lee tried one more charge at his old enemy. His men broke through Sheridan's cavalry and for a moment there was clear sky for the last stand of the tattered relics of the Army of Northern Virginia. Then line after line of Federal reinforcements appeared, and it was over. Lee the fox had been run to ground by Sheridan the hound. That same day Sheridan looked on as Lee and Grant signed the document of surrender in a parlor in Appomattox.

Sheridan's glory days were ended, at least for a time. Sent to command the 5th Military District (Texas and Louisiana) in 1867, he was so harsh in applying Reconstruction policy that he was recalled by President Andrew Johnson. For the next 15 years he served in various military capacities, chiefly in directing the government's agonizing and ultimately genocidal wars against the Cheyennes, Comanches, and other Indian tribes. It was Sheridan who inspired the phrase, 'The only good Indian is a dead Indian.' In 1884 he succeeded his old friend William Tecumseh Sherman as commander-in-chief of the US Army. Shortly before his death four years later he was honored with the rank of full general. Never a master of military science, he undoubtedly had a flair for leadership and for infusing his troops with his own indomitable fighting spirit. History, however, will remember him primarily, along with Sherman, as one of the first to implement the practice of total warfare.

The ruins of General Lee's headquarters at Petersburg, as depicted by A R Waud.

The charge of Sheridan at the Battle of Five Forks, Virginia.

Union soldiers at
Appomattox Court House,
Virginia, April 1865.

CODA:
GRANT AND LEE
Appomattox

On 9 April 1864 Grant, newly appointed General-in-chief of the US Army, set up his headquarters with the Army of the Potomac in Virginia. The final contest had begun. Exactly one year later, on Palm Sunday, 9 April 1865, the long and bloody struggle was over. In the sitting room of the house of Wilmer McLean in the small village of Appomattox Court House, the two greatest generals of the Civil War sat down together and agreed on the terms that would at last bring peace and unite a divided nation.

In the intervening year Lee had demonstrated, against overwhelming odds, his superb skill in strategy and tactics. In the Wilderness, at Spotsylvania and Cold Harbor, his dwindling, half-starved, ragged army held off the mighty Moloch of the North, possessed of unbounded resources and well-fed, well-equipped troops to throw into the effort to win and win at all costs. It is reckoned that during that period Grant sacrificed three men for every one of Lee's men killed, wounded, or captured. But the long siege of Petersburg, when for months the Confederate soldiers eked out a wretched existence in muddy trenches, subjected to continual mortar and artillery fire from Union batteries, decimated the once proud Army of Northern Virginia to a pathetic remnant of what it had been. At last Petersburg had to be abandoned and Richmond evacuated. One option remained to Lee – to pull his weary men away to the West and join up with Joseph Johnston's small force in North Carolina. But it was not to be; Sheridan and his cavalry saw to that. Word got through about the direction Lee was taking, and all his escape routes were cut off. When, on 7 April, Grant sent Lee a letter suggesting that further resistance was hopeless, Lee knew the time had come to start negotiating the terms of surrender.

No surrender of one general to another has ever been so poignant as that at Appomattox. For it was, essentially, neither victory nor defeat. Although it can hardly be said that the two men were, in background and temperament, 'brothers,' both wanted above all peace for their country, united or divided. The contrast in appearance between the two was striking: Grant, an unimposing five feet eight inches in height, with stooped shoulders, looking rather grubby in the plain attire of a private with only a pair of shoulder straps to indicate his rank, his boots spattered with mud; Lee, six feet in height, erect, resplendent in a uniform of Confederate gray, replete with sword, clean top-boots with spurs, and long buckskin gloves. (It so happened that Lee had literally nothing else to wear – a few days before all baggage had had to be destroyed, except for what each man wore on his back, so naturally they had all saved out their newest suits.) Yet in their respectful attitude toward one another, in Grant's generosity about the terms of surrender, in Lee's dignified conduct of a painful act, each had his noblest hour.

When the war ended Grant was 42 and his star

Previous page, left: Onlookers weep as the Confederate battle flag is furled for the last time.

Previous page, right: The surrender of Lee.

Above: Robert E Lee after Appomatox.

Left: A portrait of Ulysses S Grant surrounded by scenes from his command.

at its zenith. In 1868 he was elected president of the United States and served two terms – marked, regrettably, by scandal and corruption, for which he was responsible primarily by inattention and

gullibility. After a two-year world tour, he made the mistake of letting himself be talked into investing his entire wealth in what seemed an enterprising business venture. The venture failed disastrously; once again, as in his earlier attempts at business, he was completely wiped out. At that point Samuel L Clemens, better known as Mark Twain, came to the rescue. He was chief owner of a publishing firm and proposed that Grant write his memoirs, for which he would receive a substantial advance. Grant began the task on 21 February 1885. He was already suffering severely from cancer of the throat – the result, doctors would say today, of smoking 20 to 25 cigars a day for years. Unable to dictate because his voice failed, he wrote in pencil on a writing tablet in his lap. The last chapter was complete a week before his death five months later. The book earned $450,000 in royalties for his widow. Though far from a literary masterpiece, Grant's memoirs rank among the major military narratives of history.

For Lee at the war's end, the future looked bleak. He was nearing 60, his property was gone, the only career for which he had been trained and knew was lost to him forever. Offers came to him, of course, because of the luster of his name – from insurance companies and other industrial enterprises, even from abroad. He declined them all. Then came one offer he could not decline – from a small, down-at-the-heels college in Lexington, Virginia. The trustees of Washington College

asked him to be its president at a salary of $1500 a year. It was an opportunity to help shape a new generation to be responsible citizens of a nation. Lee transformed the small college into one of the outstanding educational institutions of the South. The year following his death in 1870, its name was changed to Washington and Lee University. His tomb is in the university's chapel, not far from the final resting place of his beloved and most trusted lieutenant, Stonewall Jackson.

Top: The scene of surrender. Sheridan stands to Lee's left, and Meade to Grant's left.

Above: McLean House, Appomatox Court House, Virginia.

Acknowledgments

The author and publisher would like to thank the following people who helped in the preparation of this book: Mike and Sue Rose, who designed it; Donna Cornell, who did the picture research; and Barbara Thrasher and Elizabeth Montgomery, who edited it.

Picture Credits

Bison Picture Library: 6, 11 top & bottom left, 22 middle, 53 top, 55 top, 71, 75 bottom, 86 top, 87 bottom, 91 bottom right, 92–3 top, 98 left, 123 bottom, 131, 132 bottom, 138–9, 140, 146–7, 150–51, 153 top, 157 top, 162–3, 163 bottom, 166–7 (both), 170–71, 175 bottom, 186–7
Anne S K Brown Military Collection, Brown University Library: 4–5, 9 bottom, 10 (both), 12, 13, 14–15, 16, 20, 22–3, top, 24–5, 27, 33 bottom, 36, 37 bottom right, 40, 43 (both), 44–5, 54, 56–7, 58–9, 61, 70–71, 73 (both), 77, 78-9 (all), 80 top & bottom right, 82–3 (both), 84 (both), 85 top, 86 bottom, 87 top, 90, 91 bottom left, 93 bottom, 97 top left, 99, 100 top, 101, 102–03 (both), 108 top, 114, 115, 126–7, 134–5 (both), 137 (both), 141, 144 (both), 153 bottom, 155, 156, 157 bottom, 163 top, 170 top, 171 top, 173 top, 174–5, 175 bottom, 176–7, 179, 181, 182–3, 188 bottom
Chicago Historical Society: 29, 35 top, 55 left, 64–5, 81, 143 top, 148, 152, 189 bottom
Rutherford B Hayes Presidential Center: 9 top, 17 left, 22 bottom, 34 (both), 46 top, 47 top, 110, 113, 123 right, top, 128 top, 130 bottom, 145 bottom
Ian Hogg: 23 bottom left, 37 bottom right, 128 bottom, 132 top two
Library of Congress: 7, 8 bottom, 17 top & bottom right, 18, 19, 21, 23 right, 28–9, 30, 31 (both), 32, 33 top, 35 bottom, 41 (both), 42, 45, 48–9, 50, 52, 53 bottom, 56, 60 (both), 63 (both), 66–7, 67, 69 (both), 75 top, 76, 80, 85 bottom, 89 bottom, 92, 93 top right, 97 top right, 98 right, 100 bottom, 104–05 (both), 109, 112–13, 116–17, 118, 119 (both), 121, 129 bottom, 136, 142 top, 143 bottom, 145 top, 149, 158 bottom, 160–61 (all), 164 top, 164–5, 168, 169, 173 bottom two, 180 (both), 184–5, 187, 188 top, 189 top
Museum of the Confederacy: 37 top, 62, 88–9 top, 130 top
National Archives: 68, 72, 97 bottom, 142 bottom, 151, 154
Courtesy of the Beverly R Robinson Collection, Naval Academy Museum: 94–5
Naval Photographic Center, Washington, DC: 124–5, 164 bottom
Peter Newark's Western Americana: 2–3, 91 top, 120–21, 122–3, 133
New York Public Library Picture Collection: 8 top, 26, 38–9, 46 bottom, 47 bottom, 88 top left, 88–9 bottom center, 108 bottom, 111 (both), 158 top, 178
US Army Photograph: 172
US Naval Historical Center: 96
Virginia Military Institute: 106-07
Virginia State Library: 51, 129 top